PHYSICS
FOR KIDS

49
Easy Experiments
with Electricity
and Magnetism

Robert W. Wood

Illustrations by Steve Hoeft

TAB BOOKS

Blue Ridge Summit, PA

FIRST EDITION
FOURTH PRINTING

Library of Congress Cataloging-in-Publication Data

Wood, Robert W., 1933 –
    Physics for kids : 49 easy experiments with electricity and magnetism / by Robert W. Wood.
       p.   cm.
    Summary: Describes forty-nine simple experiments involving electricity or magnetism, including ''How to Make a Flashlight,'' ''How to Make a Rheostat,'' and ''How to Destroy a Magnet.''
    ISBN 0-8306-8412-3   ISBN 0-8306-3412-6 (pbk.)
    1. Electricity—Experiments—Juvenile literature.   2. Magnetism-
-Experiments—Juvenile literature. [1. Electricity—Experiments.
2. Magnetism—Experiments.   3. Experiments.]   I. Title.
QC527.2.W66   1990
537'.078—dc20   89-48458
                                    CIP
                                     AC

Acquisitions Editor: Kimberly Tabor
Book Editor: Lori Flaherty
Director of Production: Katherine G. Brown
Paperbound cover photograph by Susan Riley, Harrisonburg, VA   SFK

Contents

Introduction

Physics is the science of natural things and occurrences. It deals with properties, changes, and interactions of matter and energy. Prehistoric man first applied the laws of physics when he put rollers under a heavy load and discovered that it was easier to pull. Early Greek philosophers, the great thinkers of their time, proposed that the Earth was a sphere and guessed that an eclipse occurred when the Earth blocked the sun's rays. Around 400 B.C., one philosopher taught that matter was made up of tiny particles he called atoms. During the 200s B.C., the laws of the lever were discovered along with the principles of the weight of floating bodies. During the Middle Ages, however, few people were interested in physics, and little progress was made for hundreds of years. Fortunately, in the 1200s and 1400s, people such as Roger Bacon and Leonardo da Vinci began to see the importance of physics, and by the mid-1500s, the study was reborn.

Today, physics is such a broad and fascinating science that it is divided into several fields to better understand it—mechanics, heat, optics, electricity and magnetism, and sound. These studies sometimes overlap, however. For instance, someone studying mechanics might need to understand heat because of the friction of moving parts, or a student of electricity might need to study optics to better understand photo cells. Students studying electricity and magnetism to learn why a telephone worked would also have to learn how sound waves vibrate objects that send electrical signals.

This book opens the door to one of the most exciting worlds of physics—the science of electricty and magnetism. Everything is basically electrical. All matter is made up of atoms, and each atom has one or more electrons and one or more protons. The electron is a negative particle of electricity and the proton is a positive particle of electricity. They each have equal, but opposite, charges of electricity. The protons are much heavier, so they are bound tightly to the center of the atoms. This means only electrons can move freely. Normally, atoms have an equal number of electrons and protons. This makes them neutral, but if an atom gains some electrons it becomes negatively charged. If it loses electrons, it becomes positively charged. Atoms with the same charges repel each other, but if they have different charges, they attract each other. A negative charge repels another negative charge and a positive charge repels another positive charge. But a negative charge is attracted to a positive charge.

Often, many people think that there are two kinds of electricity— static electricity and current electricity. Actually, they are really the same. The difference is that the electrons are not moving in static electricity, while current electricity is made up of moving electrons. When electrons move and produce an electrical current, they develop a magnetic field. To understand electricity, it is important to know something about the relationship of electricity and magnetism. The two subjects are closely related. Electricity can produce magnetism and magnetism can produce electricity. Understanding their relationship has led to the development of most of today's entertaining and labor-saving devices, and only our imaginations are the limit to the exciting discoveries in the future.

The experiments in this book are an easy introduction into the study of electricity and magnetism. You'll learn what electricity and magnetism are, where they come from, and some of the ways you can use them.

Be sure to read the *Symbols Used in This Book* section that follows before you begin any experiments. It warns you of all the safety precautions you should consider before you begin a project and whether or not you should have a teacher or parent help you. Keep safety in mind, and you are sure to have a rewarding first experience in the fascinating world of physics.

Although it is not necessary, I would advise you to do the experiments in order because some of the principles of electricity and magnetism you learn in the first few experiments will help you to do later experiments.

Symbols Used in This Book

Carefully look over the symbols key below before beginning any experiment. These symbols mean that you should use extra safety precautions, or that some experiments require adult supervision. Before proceeding, *always* refer to this key whenever you see a warning symbol.

Science experiments can be fun and exciting, but safety should always be a first consideration. Parents and teachers are encouraged to participate with their children and students. Adult supervision is advised for very young children. Use common sense and make safety the first consideration, and you will have a safe, fun, educational, and rewarding experience.

 Materials or tools used in this experiment could be dangerous in young hands. Adult supervision is recommended. Children should be instructed on the care and handling of sharp tools or combustible or toxic materials and how to protect surfaces.

 Exercise caution around any open flame or very hot surface such as a stove or hot plate. Adult supervision recommended. Children should be instructed on how to handle hot materials and protect clothing, hair, and surfaces.

 Electricity is used in this experiment. Young children should be supervised and older children cautioned about the hazards of electricity.

 Protective safety goggles should be worn to protect against shattering glass or other hazards that could damage the eyes.

ELECTRICITY
AND
MAGNETISM

Experiment 1

Materials

- ☐ hard rubber or nylon comb
- ☐ piece of unsweetened dry cereal (puffed rice)
- ☐ length of sewing thread (about two feet long)
- ☐ piece of wool cloth or a heavy crop of clean, dry hair

Understanding Static Electricity

Wash the comb with warm, soapy water to remove any oil, then shake off any drops of water. Tie one end of the thread to the piece of puffed rice as shown in Fig. 1-1. Tie the other end of the thread to a support so that the cereal is free to swing like a pendulum (Fig. 1-2). Rub the comb briskly with the wool cloth and slowly bring one end of the

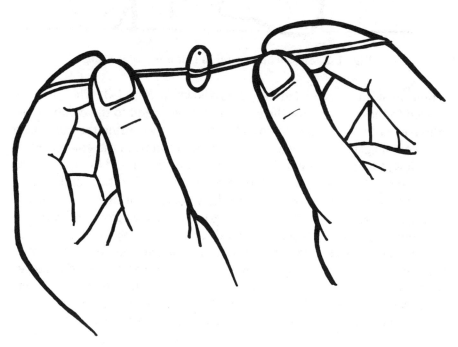

Fig. 1-1. *Tie the cereal to one end of the thread.*

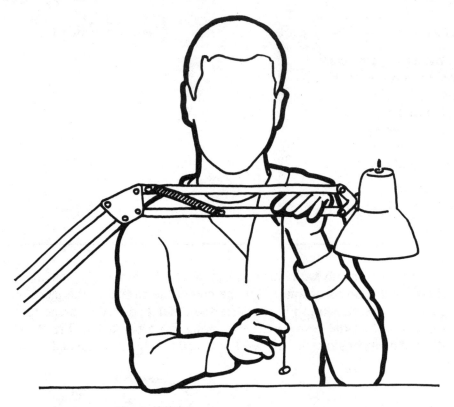

Fig. 1-2. *Suspend the cereal so that it is free to swing.*

comb near the suspended cereal as shown in Fig. 1-3. The cereal is pulled to the comb. Allow the cereal to stay attached to the comb. Soon, the piece of cereal will jump from the comb. Slowly bring the comb near the cereal again. The piece of cereal tries to run from the comb (Fig. 1-4). Now, touch the cereal with the tip of your finger and bring the comb near the cereal. Once again, the cereal is attracted to the comb.

When the comb was rubbed by the wool cloth, it built up a negative charge of electricity. It picked up extra electrons from the wool. A charged object attracts an uncharged, or neutral, object. The piece of cereal did not have a charge so it was attracted to the comb. But while the cereal was touching the comb, some of the extra electrons moved from the comb to the cereal. Soon, it also built up a negative charge. Because both the comb and the cereal are now negatively charged, they push each other away. When you touched the cereal, the surplus elec-

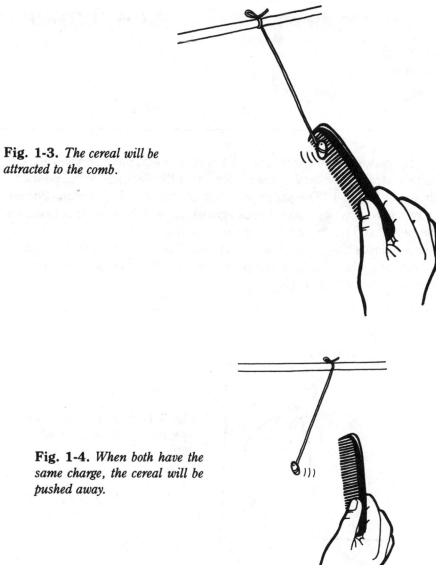

Fig. 1-3. *The cereal will be attracted to the comb.*

Fig. 1-4. *When both have the same charge, the cereal will be pushed away.*

trons moved from the cereal to your finger. The cereal loses its charge and is again attracted to the comb.

Experiments with static electricity work best when the air is dry. On humid days, the charge leaks off into the moisture in the air.

Experiment 2

Electrically Charged Newspaper

Materials

☐ wooden pencil
☐ newspaper page

Spread the newspaper against a wall. Smooth out the wrinkles and quickly stroke it several times all over with the flat side of the pencil as shown in Fig. 2-1. The paper will stick to the wall. Peel up one corner and let it go. It will be pulled back against the wall. The friction between the pencil and the paper develop an electrical charge in the paper. This charge causes the paper to be attracted to the wall. If the air in the room is very dry when you peel the paper off, you might be able to hear the crackle of the static charges.

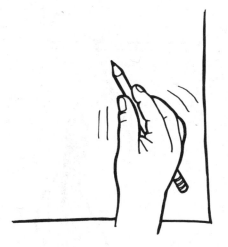

Fig. 2-1. *Stroke the newspaper with the pencil to build up a charge.*

Experiment 3

Dancing Dolls

Cut out a few tiny doll figures from the tissue paper. The figures should be a little shorter than the thickness of the books. Place the books on a table about six inches apart to form a support for the glass (Fig. 3-1). Scatter the figures in the space between the books and rest the glass on top of the books as shown in Figs. 3-1 and 3-2. Rub the glass vigorously with the nylon cloth and the figures begin to dance and move about.

When the glass was rubbed with the nylon cloth, the friction caused electrons to move from the glass to the nylon. The nylon built up a negative charge. Because the glass lost some electrons, it no longer had a balance between electrons and protons. The excess of protons causes the glass to become positively charged.

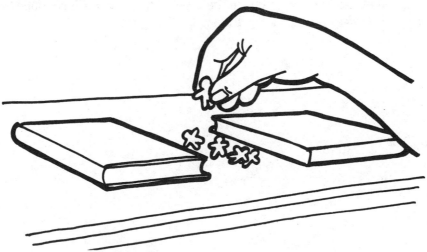

Fig. 3-1. *Place the figures between two books.*

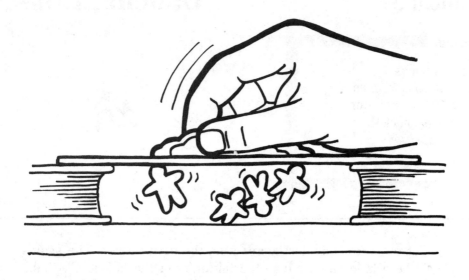

Fig. 3-2. *Rub the glass with a piece of nylon to make the figures dance.*

The atoms in the tissue dolls are equally balanced, so the dolls are neutral. This makes them attracted to the charged glass. But when they touch the glass, they lose some electrons. They begin to build up a positive charge and are soon pushed away from the positive charge of the glass. When the dolls separate from the glass, they pick up electrons from the atoms in the air and become neutral. Then they are again attracted to the positive charge in the glass. This action will continue as long as the glass has extra electrons.

Experiment 4

An Electrostatic Airplane

Materials

- ☐ piece of aluminum foil
- ☐ plastic rod
- ☐ wool cloth
- ☐ scissors

Cut the aluminum foil into the shape of an airplane. Briskly rub the plastic rod with the wool cloth to build up a charge in the rod. Move the rod near the airplane. The airplane will jump to the rod then jump away (Figs. 4-1 and 4-2). The airplane is repelled by the rod. With a little practice, you can keep the airplane in the air by maneuvering the charged rod.

Rubbing the rod with wool caused the rod to be charged with static electricity. When the rod touches the airplane, the airplane also became charged. The two charges were alike so the airplane and the rod repelled each other.

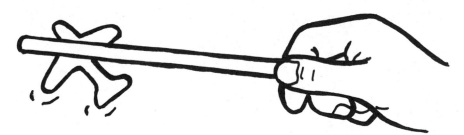

Fig. 4-1. *The airplane will be attracted to the rod.*

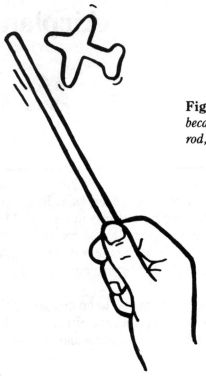

Fig. 4-2. *When the airplane became charged the same as the rod, it was pushed away.*

Experiment 5

Static Electricity Light

Materials

☐ flourescent tube from a
fluorescent lamp
☐ piece of wool
☐ dark room

Make sure the lamp is turned off and unplugged. Then carefully remove the tube from a flourescent lamp or ask an adult for help (Fig. 5-1). Take it into a dark room. Vigorously rub the tube with the wool cloth as shown in Fig. 5-2. The tube will try to light.

The friction between the wool and the glass tube caused electrons to strike and dislodge electrons from atoms in the gas inside the tube. When these dislodged electrons try to get back into their atoms, they give off ultraviolet rays. These rays strike a phosphor coating on the inside of the glass tube, which causes the coating to glow and give off light.

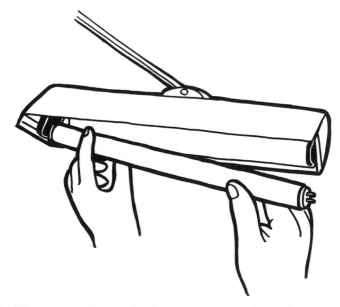

Fig. 5-1. *Flourescent tubes can be dangerous. Ask for help when removing them from a lamp.*

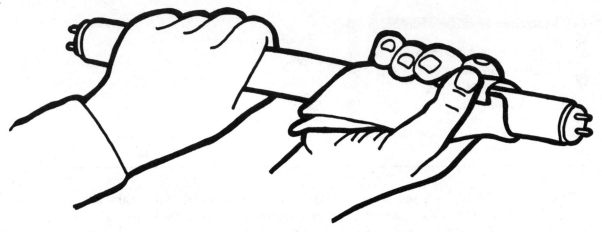

Fig. 5-2. *Rub the tube with a piece of wool and it will try to light.*

Experiment 6

How to Make an Electroscope

Materials

- ☐ glass jug (32 oz. ketchup bottle or 16 oz. salad dressing bottle)
- ☐ cork to fit the bottle
- ☐ heavy copper wire (about nine inches long)
- ☐ 2 strips of aluminum foil (about 1 1/2 × 1/4 inches)
- ☐ ball of aluminum foil (about the size of a marble)
- ☐ comb
- ☐ piece of wool
- ☐ pliers to bend wire
- ☐ candle and matches
- ☐ newspaper
- ☐ tongs

The copper wire should be bare. You can purchase it at most hardware stores. Otherwise, you might have to strip the insulation from a piece of scrap wire. When removing insulation, place the wire on a board or some other wooden surface. Never use your knee for a work bench. One slip of the knife and you will surely receive a bad cut. If you are unsure, ask an adult for help. Once you have the bare wire, force one end through the cork as shown in Fig 6-1. Let it stick through the cork about an inch. Bend about 1 1/2 inches of the other end of the wire at a right angle (Fig. 6-2). Bend this 1 1/2 inch part in half so that if folds back horizontally against itself (Fig. 6-3). This should form a narrow horizontal "U" with the sides nearly touching.

You need to seal the point where the wire enters and leaves the cork. Have an adult light the candle and apply wax to the cork to make a good seal. Be sure to lay down newspaper first because hot wax could burn some tabletops (Fig. 6-4). Attach the aluminum strips to the wire by folding one end on each strip over each bend (Fig. 6-5).

Without the cork in the bottle, carefully heat the bottle over the can-

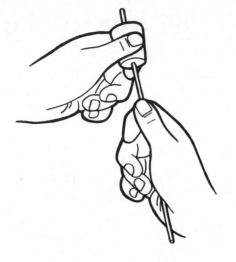

Fig. 6-1. *Force the copper wire through the cork.*

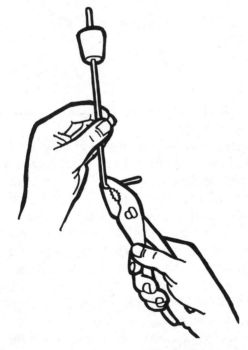

Fig. 6-2. *Bend the wire at a right angle.*

dle using tongs (Fig. 6-6). This causes the air inside to expand and removes some of the moisture. While the bottle is warm, carefully lower the wire and aluminum strips into the bottle. Press the cork tightly in place and allow the bottle to cool. The aluminum strips should be suspended at least one inch from the bottom as shown in Fig. 6-7. Finally,

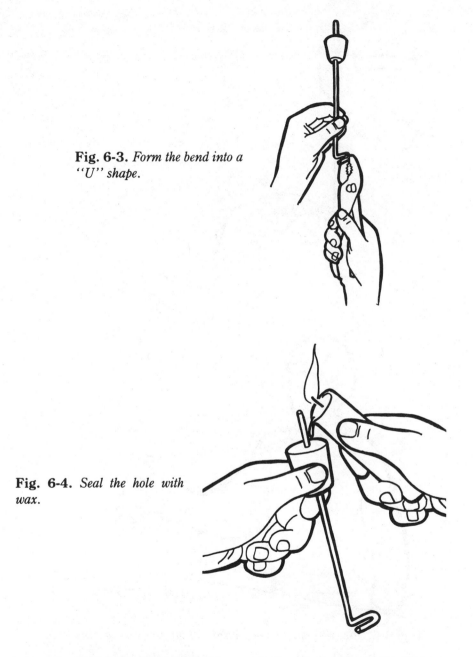

Fig. 6-3. *Form the bend into a "U" shape.*

Fig. 6-4. *Seal the hole with wax.*

press the ball of aluminum foil to the one-inch end of copper wire sticking through the cork. This completes the electroscope

Rub the comb with the wool to built up a charge. Slowly bring one end of the comb near the ball of aluminum being careful not to touch the

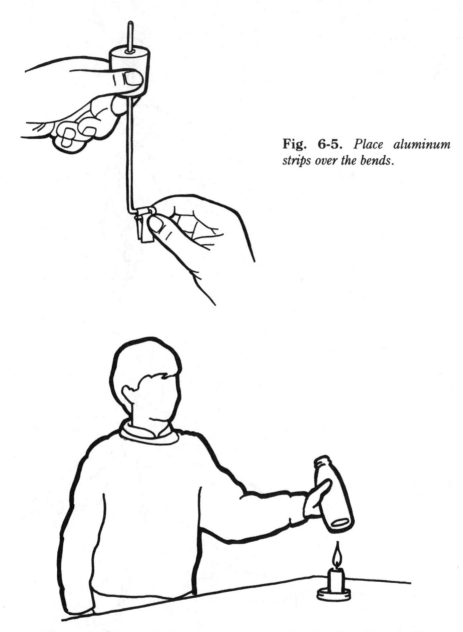

Fig. 6-5. *Place aluminum strips over the bends.*

Fig. 6-6. *Heat the bottle to remove some of the air and moisture inside.*

ball (Fig. 6-8). Watch the aluminum strips, and they will move apart. Electrons moved from the comb, down the wire, and charged the aluminum strips. The strips have an excess of electrons so they both have a negative charge and repel each other. Take the comb away, and the strips

Fig. 6-7. *Press the ball of aluminum on the end of the wire.*

will gradually fall back again as the surplus of electrons travel back up the wire and leak into the air.

A glass rod rubbed with a piece of silk will produce the same effect except the strips will have a positive charge. The glass attracted electrons from the strips leaving them with an excess of protons. An excess of protons creates a positive charge. Try testing the polarity of other static charges. Begin by charging the electroscope with wool and the comb. This charges it negatively. When you bring a charged object near the ball and the strips continue to spread apart, you know the object also has a negative charge. But if the object causes the strips to move together, the object has a positive charge.

Fig. 6-8. *Bring a charged comb near the ball and the strips will separate.*

Experiment 7
The Potato Battery

Insert one end of the steel wire into one end of the potato and stick one end of the copper wire into the other end of the potato. Connect the negative probe of the meter to the steel wire (see Fig. 7-1). Connect the positive probe of the meter to the copper wire. The meter should read about 1/2 volt. A lemon, or a small glass of lemon juice can be substituted for the potato.

Try moving the two wires closer together to see if the voltage changes. The voltage exists because of the chemical action of the potato and the steel and copper wire.

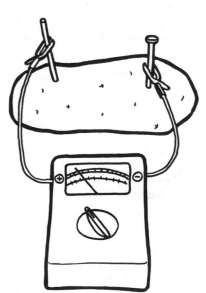

Fig. 7-1. *A volt meter will show about 1/2 volt.*

Experiment 8

Penny and Dime Battery

Materials

- ☐ lemon juice or vinegar
- ☐ piece of paper towel or blotter
- ☐ equal number of pennies and dimes
- ☐ dc voltmeter

Use lemon juice or mix a tablespoon of vinegar with a glass of water. Then soak the paper towel in the solution. Tear it into coin-size pieces. Place a penny on a table then lay a wet piece of paper towel on top (see Fig. 8-1). Place a dime on top of that, and then another piece of the paper towel. You want a stack of alternating pennies and dimes, with each coin separated by a wet piece of paper towel. Start the stack with a penny and end it with dime.

Fig. 8-1. *Place the wet piece of paper towel between the penny and the dime.*

Connect a voltmeter to the bottom penny and the top dime and it will indicate a small amount of voltage (see Fig. 8-2). In 1800, Alessandro Volta invented the voltaic pile. He discovered that if you immerse two unlike metals in an acid solution, you can produce a steady electric current. The lemon juice was the acid solution and the pennies and dimes were the two unlike metals. The electrical current from the pile traveled through the meter and deflected the needle, indicating the small amount of voltage.

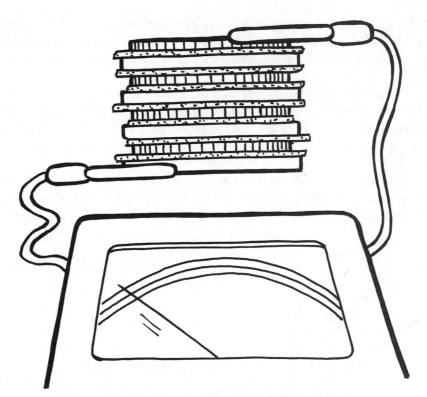

Fig. 8-2. *The stack of coins will produce a small voltage.*

Experiment 9

Current Electricity and the Electrical Circuit

Materials

- ☐ 1 1/2 volt battery
- ☐ 1 1/2 volt flashlight bulb
- ☐ length of flexible copper wire (about 12 inches long)

A good source of copper wire for experiments is to carefully strip the insulation from an old lamp cord. The wires inside are stranded and easy to work with. Have an adult carefully strip away the insulation for you.

Twist one end of the copper wire tightly around the metal part of the light bulb. Stand the battery upright on a table with the bottom of the battery resting on the other end of the copper wire. Touch the metal point on the bottom of the bulb to the top of the battery, and the bulb will light (see Fig. 9-1). Remove the bulb and the light goes out.

The top of the battery and the center point on the bottom of the bulb is taking the place of the switch in an electrical circuit. When you touched the bulb to the battery, you closed the switch. The light bulb is

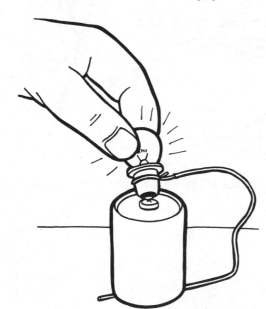

Fig. 9-1. *The electrical circuit must be complete for current to flow.*

22

considered the circuit load and the battery is the power source. In order for electricity to flow, (an electric current) there must be a closed path. When the light burned, current flowed out the bottom of the battery, through the wire to the side of the bulb. Then it traveled through the filament inside the bulb, out the bottom of the bulb and back into the top of the battery. This makes a closed path or electric circuit. Any break along the circuit will stop the current and the light will not burn.

Experiment 10

How to Make a Flashlight

Remove about two inches of insulation from each end of the wire. Twist one end of the wire tightly around the metal sides of the bulb and make a coil of wire at the other end as shown in Fig. 10-1. Tape the coiled end to the bottom of the battery. Bend the wire up the side of the battery and fasten it in place with tape. Bend the wire at the top of the battery so that the bottom of the bulb can touch the positive terminal of the battery (Fig. 10-2). Press the top bend in the wire so that the bottom of the bulb contacts the battery. The bulb will light, release pressure on the wire and the bulb goes out (Fig. 10-3).

Fig. 10-1. *Connect a small wire to a flashlight bulb.*

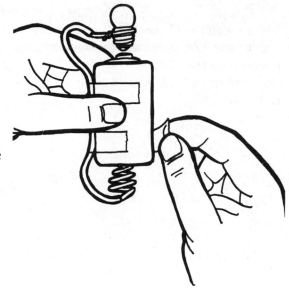

Fig. 10-2. *Tape the wire to a battery.*

Fig. 10-3. *The bulb will light when the bottom touches the battery.*

Electrons flowed from the bottom of the battery through the wire, and through the filament of the bulb down to the top of the battery. The circuit was complete and the bulb burned. When the pressure was released on the bent wire, the bulb became disconnected from the battery and the circuit opened. The electrons couldn't flow and the bulb could not light.

Experiment 11

Testing for a Steady Hand

Materials

- ☐ six-volt battery
- ☐ six-volt bell or buzzer
- ☐ screw eye or loop of wire
- ☐ two feet of stiff wire (coat hanger with paint sanded off)
- ☐ wooden pencil
- ☐ heavy book
- ☐ transparent tape
- ☐ insulated copper wire (about four feet of bell wire)

Cut about a 12-inch length of copper wire and remove about a half inch of insulation from each end. Tie one end tightly around one end of the stiff wire. Place this end on the edge of a table. Extend the stiff wire over the edge and hold it in place with the book (see Fig. 11-1). Connect the free end of the copper wire to one of the terminals of the battery. Cut another short length of copper wire and remove the insulation from each end. Connect one end to the other terminal of the battery and one terminal on the bell. Remove the insulation from each end of the remaining length of copper wire. Connect one end to the other terminal of the bell. Twist the other end around the screw eye or form the bare end of the wire into a small loop. Extend this from the end of the pencil and fasten it in place with tape. Run the wire down one side of the pencil and hold it in place with tape (see Fig. 11-2). Now try to slide the loop over the length of stiff wire and back off again without the loop touching the stiff wire. The bell will ring each time the loop touches the wire.

The loop and the stiff wire are the ends of the electrical circuit. When one comes in contact with the other, the current flows from the battery and causes the bell to ring.

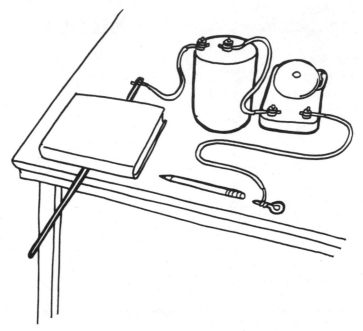

Fig. 11-1. *Connect the wire, the battery, and the bell together.*

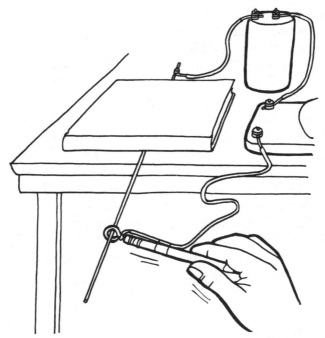

Fig. 11-2. *When the screw eye touches the wire, the bell will ring.*

Experiment 12

Materials

- ☐ 1 1/2 volt battery
- ☐ 1 1/2 volt flashlight bulb
- ☐ flexible copper wire (about 12 inches long)
- ☐ pencil
- ☐ sheet of paper
- ☐ paper clip

Conductors and Insulators

Set up the circuit as explained in experiment 9. Then touch one end of the paper clip to the top of the battery. Touch the bottom of the light bulb to the other end of the paper clip as shown in Fig. 12-1. Notice how bright the bulb burns. Now place the point of the pencil on top of the battery. Position it so that the width of the pencil lead will make the connection. Touch the bulb to the lead (Fig. 12-2). Notice that the bulb burns, but not as bright. Separate the battery and the bulb with a slip of

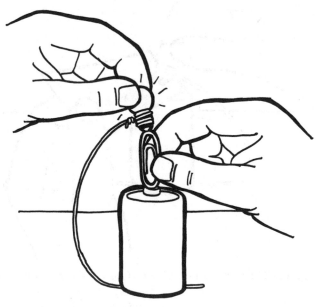

Fig. 12-1. *A paper clip is a good conductor.*

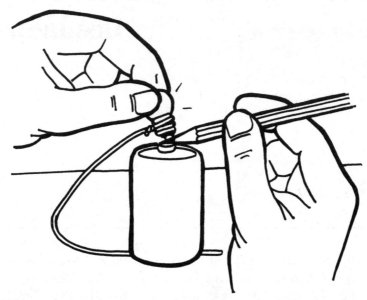

Fig. 12-2. *Pencil lead will conduct electricity, but not very well.*

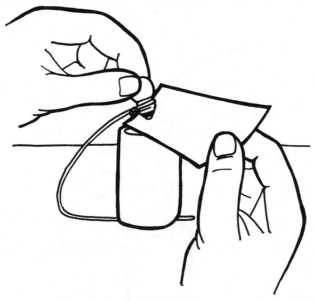

Fig. 12-3. *Paper is an insulator. It does not conduct electricity.*

paper and the bulb will not light at all (see Fig. 12-3). This shows that metal is a good conductor. Pencil lead (graphite) does conduct electricity, but not as well as metal, and paper does not conduct at all. Paper is an insulator.

Experiment 13

How to Make a Rheostat

Materials

- ☐ flashlight battery
- ☐ flashlight bulb
- ☐ full length of pencil lead from mechanical pencil
- ☐ thin copper wire
- ☐ transparent tape

Connect one end of the wire to the top of the battery and fasten it in place with tape (Fig. 13-1). Twist the other end of the wire tightly around the metal side of the bulb (Fig. 13-2). Place the pencil lead on a flat surface and rest the bottom of the battery on one end of the lead. Now touch the bottom of the bulb to the lead close to the battery as shown in Fig. 13-3. Notice the brightness of the bulb. Gradually slide the bulb down the length of the lead as shown in Fig. 13-4. The bulb

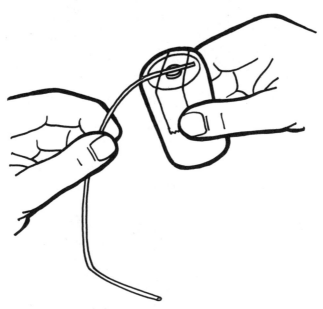

Fig. 13-1. *Attach the wire to the top of the battery.*

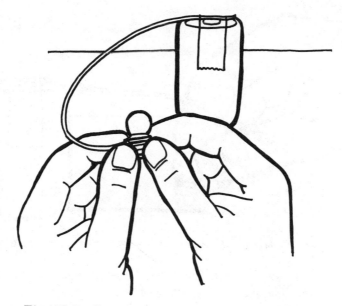

Fig. 13-2. *Connect the other end of the wire to the bulb.*

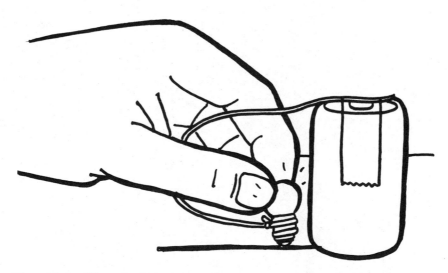

Fig. 13-3. *When the bulb is placed on the lead close to the battery, it burns brightly.*

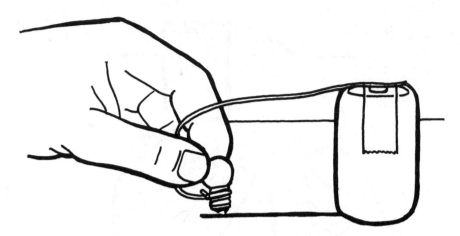

Fig. 13-4. *The bulb becomes dimmer as it is moved away from the battery.*

slowly glows dimmer. The pencil lead is not a good conductor and makes a good rheostat. The greater the distance between the battery and the bulb, the weaker the current becomes. A rheostat is a variable resistor used to control current.

Experiment 14

How Fuses Protect a Circuit

Materials

- [ ] 4 or 5 flashlight batteries or a lantern battery
- [ ] old lamp cord with plug (about 18 inches long)
- [ ] aluminum foil
- [ ] scissors
- [ ] cardboard tube from paper towels

Separate the two halves of the lamp cord (Fig. 14-1) and trim about 1/4 inch of the insulation from each end. Slide the batteries into the cardboard tube with all of them pointing in the same direction as shown in Fig. 14-2. This aligns them in a series, the positive terminal of one battery touching the negative end of the next battery. The cardboard keeps them from rolling around.

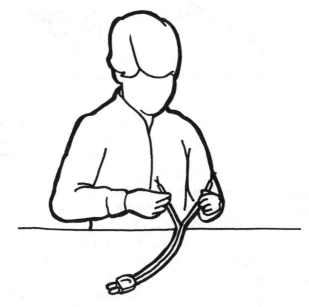

Fig. 14-1. *Separate the two halves of an old lamp cord.*

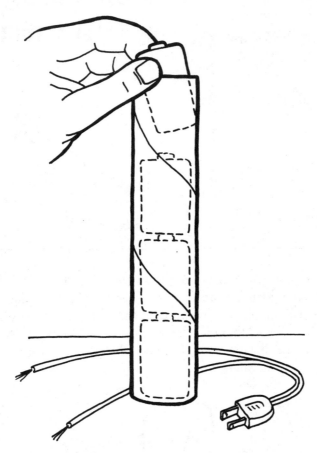

Fig. 14-2. *Place the batteries in the cardboard tube.*

Cut a very thin sliver of aluminum foil about three or four inches long (Fig. 14-3). Try to cut it as narrow as you can. This will be the fuse. Wrap one end of the aluminum foil snugly around one of the prongs of the plug. Then wrap the other end around the other prong (Fig. 14-4). When the fuse is in place, touch one end of the cord to one end of the batteries and watch the fuse as you briefly touch the other end of the cord to the other end of the batteries (Fig. 14-5). The fuse should burn in two. If not, try a thinner strip of aluminum foil.

A normal electrical circuit has a power source and a load such as a light bulb or appliance. The load is a form of resistance. This keeps the current from getting too high and starting a fire or other damage. If the

Fig. 14-3. *Cut a thin sliver from a piece of aluminum foil. This is the fuse.*

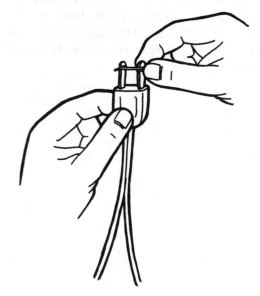

Fig. 14-4. *Wrap the thin strip of aluminum foil around the prongs on the plug.*

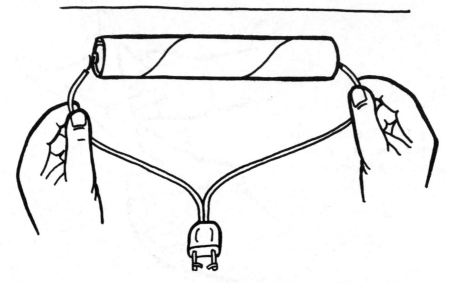

Fig. 14-5. *Connect the wires to the batteries and the fuse will burn in two.*

load or somewhere in the circuit develops a problem that causes the current to increase too much, however, the fuse burns out and stops the flow of electricity. This happens because the fuse will only allow a certain amount of current to flow. It is designed to be the weakest link in the circuit.

Experiment 15

How Wires Give Off Light

Materials

- ☐ 5 flashlight batteries or a lantern battery
- ☐ cardboard tube from paper towels
- ☐ old lamp cord with plug (about 18 inches long)
- ☐ thin, steel wire (about four inches long)
- ☐ clear drinking glass
- ☐ dark room

Separate the two halves of the lamp cord and strip about 1/4 inch of the insulation from each end. Slide the batteries into the cardboard tube and point them all in the same direction as in Experiment 14.

Separate one of the strands of a picture frame wire. Cut off about a four inch length. Tightly twist one of the ends around one of the prongs on the plug. Fasten the other end of the wire to the other prong the same way (Fig. 15-1). The wire should form a loop between the two prongs. Lower the plug about half way into the glass as shown in Fig. 15-2. This helps keep air drafts from cooling the wire. Bend the cord at the rim of the glass so that the plug will stay in position. Now, turn out the room light and touch the ends of the cord to each end of the tube of batteries. The wire will get hot and begin to glow. Soon the wire will get hot enough that it will probably break. This is because of the air in the glass. In a regular light bulb, the inside is filled with nitrogen (a gas used as a cooling agent) and the wire doesn't burn. The wire, or filament, is also made of tungsten. Tungsten is used because it can get white hot without melting. The filament is very thin because it takes less heat than a larger wire to make it glow.

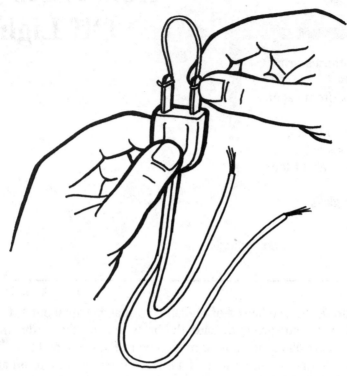

Fig. 15-1. *Connect a thin steel wire to the prongs of the plug.*

Fig. 15-2. *Connect the wires to the batteries and the wire will glow.*

Experiment 16

Materials

- ☐ 3 batteries with screw or snap terminals
- ☐ copper wire
- ☐ dc voltmeter

How to Connect Batteries in Series and Parallel

Stand the batteries upright in a row. Connect a wire from the negative terminal of the first battery to the positive terminal of the second battery. Connect a wire from the negative terminal of the second battery to the positive terminal of the third battery. Connect the positive lead of the voltmeter to the positive terminal of the first battery and the negative lead to the negative terminal of the third battery as shown in Fig. 16-1. The meter will read the combined voltages of the batteries. If each battery was six volts, the meter should read 18 volts. They are connected in series.

Remove the wires and connect a wire between all three positive terminals and a wire between the three negative terminals as shown in Fig. 16-2. Connect the meter to the negative and positive terminals of one of

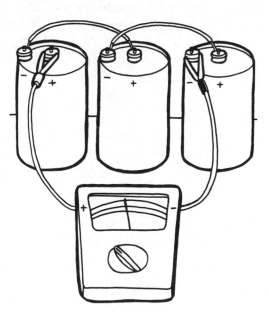

Fig. 16-1. *Batteries connected in series. If each battery supplied 6 volts, the meter would read 18 volts.*

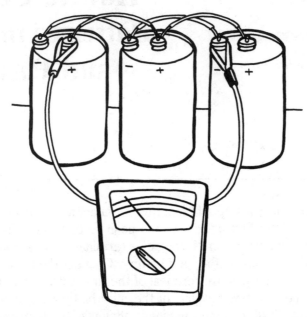

Fig. 16-2. *Batteries connected in parallel. If each battery supplied 6 volts, the meter would read 6 volts.*

the batteries. The meter will read the value of each battery. In this case, 6 volts. They are connected in parallel.

When batteries are connected in series, the useful voltage is increased with each battery. When the batteries are connected in parallel, the voltage remains the same, but the batteries are able to supply current for a longer period of time.

Experiment 17

How to Make a Transformer

Materials

- ☐ cardboard tube from paper towels
- ☐ amp meter
- ☐ battery
- ☐ 2 insulated copper wires (about four feet long)

Wind one of the wires around the tube in a neat coil—about 20 turns (Fig. 17-1). Connect the two ends to the amp meter (Fig. 17-2). This will be the secondary coil. Now wind another coil over the first (Fig. 17-3) and connect one end to one terminal on the battery. This is the primarily coil. Watch the meter and touch the other end of the coil to the

Fig. 17-1. *Wind the copper wire about 20 turns.*

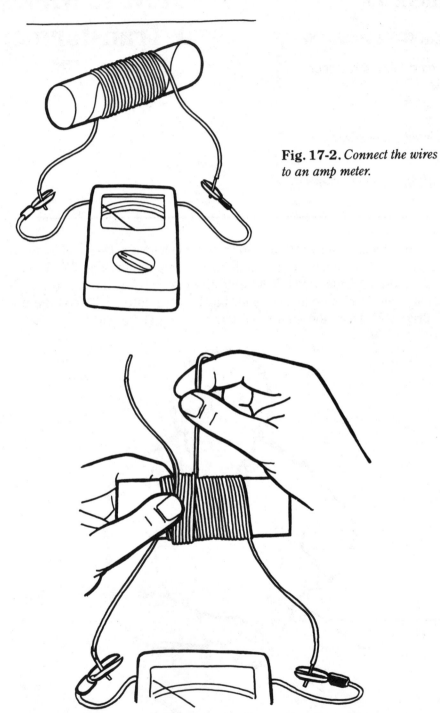

Fig. 17-2. *Connect the wires to an amp meter.*

Fig. 17-3. *Wind another coil over the first coil.*

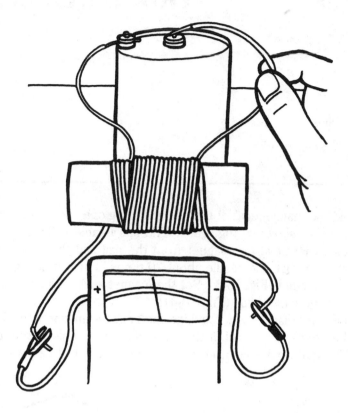

Fig. 17-4. *When current flows in one coil, it induces a current in the coil next to it.*

other terminal on the battery as shown in Fig. 17-4. The needle moves briefly then returns to rest. The battery is still connected but current is no longer flowing in the secondary coil. Watch the meter and disconnect the battery. The needle moves again but in the other direction. This happens because, when the end of the coil was touched to the battery, current flowed from the battery through the primary coil. This built up a magnetic field in the primary that, as it expanded, cut through the windings of the secondary coil. This made a current flow in the secondary coil, which made the meter move. When the magnetic field could expand no more, the current in the secondary coil stopped flowing. When the battery was disconnected, the magnetic field of the primary coil started to collapse, again cutting across the windings of the secondary coil. This caused a brief flow of current in the secondary coil but in the opposite direction.

Experiment 18   How a Magnet Works

Materials

- ☐ strong magnet
- ☐ large nail
- ☐ steel needle
- ☐ 4 or 5 paper clips

Hold the magnet against the nail and bring one end of the nail to the paper clips as shown in Fig. 18-1. The nail is able to lift some of the paper clips. Remove the magnet from the nail and the paper clips fall (Fig. 18-2). Stroke the needle about 20 times in one direction with one end of the magnet (Fig. 18-3). Set the magnet aside and use the needle to pick up the paper clips (Fig. 18-4).

When the magnet was touching the nail, the magnetic field aligned all of the atoms in the nail in the same direction. This means that the north and south poles point in the same direction. But because the nail

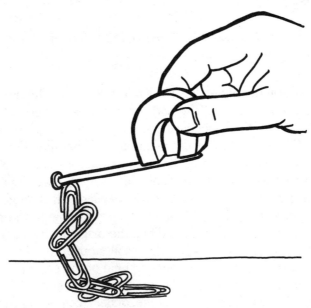

Fig. 18-1. *Soft iron, like a nail, makes a temporary magnet.*

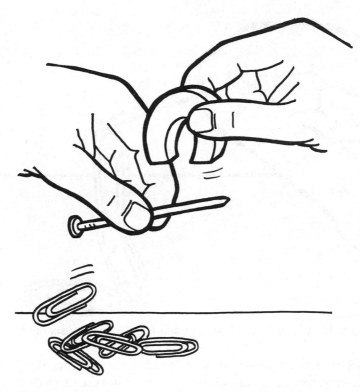

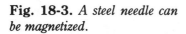

Fig. 18-2. *The nail loses it's magnetism when the permanent magnet is removed.*

Fig. 18-3. *A steel needle can be magnetized.*

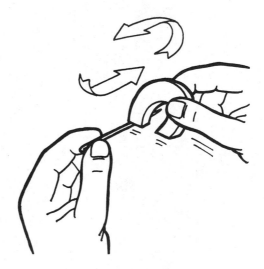

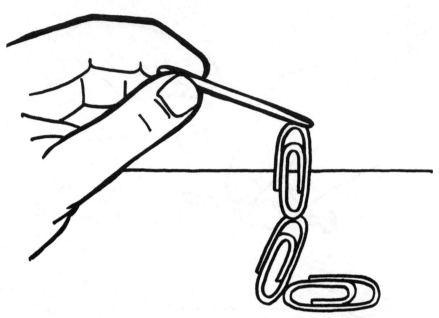

Fig. 18-4. *A steel needle is hard and keeps its magnetism longer.*

was made of iron, a softer metal, most of the atoms returned to there jumbled state when the magnet was removed, and the nail lost almost all of its magnetism. Steel is very hard. It is harder to magnetize, but it keeps its magnetic field a lot longer.

Experiment 19

How to Make a Magnet

Materials

☐ strong magnet
☐ hacksaw blade
☐ paper clips and nails

Place the hacksaw blade on the table or some other firm surface. Apply a little pressure and begin stroking the blade along its full length in one direction, using just one end of the magnet (Fig. 19-1). Lift the magnet in an arc and repeat the stroke. Slide the magnet completely past the end of the blade without stopping with smooth, steady strokes. Do this about 20 times. The hacksaw blade can now pick up the nails, paper clips, or other steel or iron pieces (Fig. 19-2).

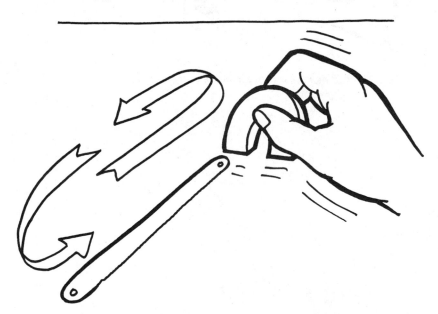

Fig. 19-1. *Stroke the hacksaw blade in one direction.*

Fig. 19-2. *The hacksaw blade has become a magnet.*

Experiment 20

How to Make a Compass

Materials

- ☐ magnet
- ☐ steel needle
- ☐ fine thread (about eight inches long)
- ☐ wooden pencil
- ☐ drinking glass
- ☐ paper (about 1 × 2 inch)

Fold the paper in the middle to make a one inch square. Thread the needle and tie a knot on the end of the thread so it won't pull through the hole. Spread the paper a little and push the needle through the center from the inside of the fold (Fig. 20-1). Gently pull the needle through the paper so that the knot is not pulled through. Remove the thread from the needle and tie the free end around the middle of the pencil. The length of the thread should suspend the paper an inch or so above the bottom of the glass as shown in Fig. 20-2. Magnetize the needle by stroking it about 20 times in one direction with one end of the magnet. Now with

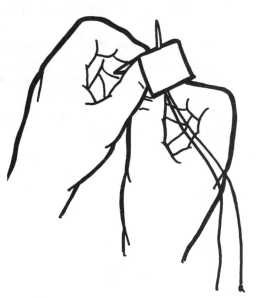

Fig. 20-1. *Push the needle through the center of the folded paper.*

51

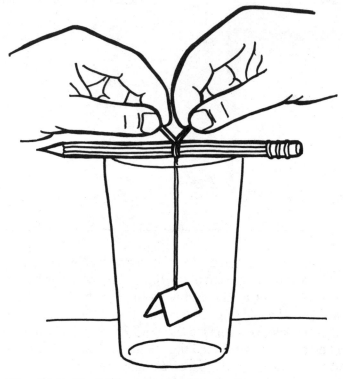

Fig. 20-2. *Tie the thread around the pencil.*

the paper spread tent-like, insert the needle horizontally through both sides of the paper. Center the needle so that it will balance (see Fig. 20-3).

Lower the needle inside the glass so that it is suspended freely by the thread and the pencil. The needle will swing a few times then align itself north and south as shown in Fig. 20-4. The earth has a huge magnetic field, with the magnetic North Pole near the geographic North Pole. One end of the needle is pointing north, but because unlike poles attract, it is the earth's North Pole attracting the south pole of the needle.

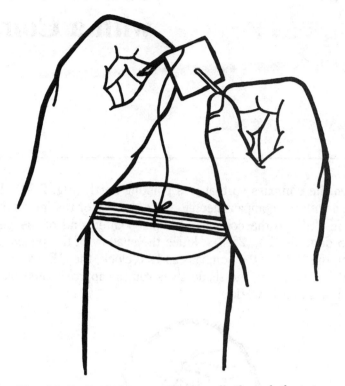

Fig. 20-3. *Push the magnetized needle through the paper.*

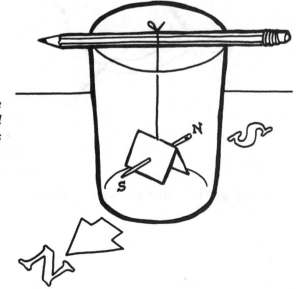

Fig. 20-4. *The needle will align itself north and south with the Earth's magnetic field.*

Experiment 21

How to Tell Time with a Compass

Materials

☐ compass
☐ pencil
☐ sunny day

Align the compass so that it is pointing north (Fig. 21-1). Line up the pencil with the compass needle. Have the eraser resting on the glass above the "S" on the compass Tilt the pointed end of the pencil up about 45 degrees (Fig. 21-2). Notice the shadow of the pencil (Fig 21-3). Using the "N" of the compass as 12 o'clock, the "E" as 3 o'clock, and "W" as 9 o'clock, the shade gives you the approximate time of day. This is how sundials work.

Fig. 21-1. *Align the compass with the needle pointing north.*

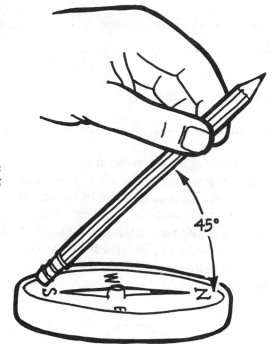

Fig. 21-2. *Place the pencil on the compass at about a 45 degree angle.*

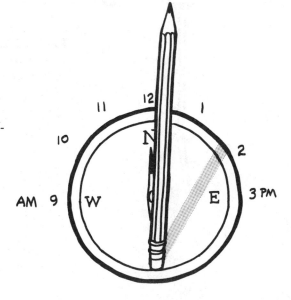

Fig. 21-3. *The shadow indicates the approximate time.*

55

Experiment 22

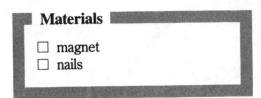

Materials

☐ magnet
☐ nails

Magnetic Induction and Polarity

Using one end of the magnet, attach the nails, end-to-end, to the magnet as shown in Fig. 22-1. The magnetic field of the magnet created a magnetic field in each nail by induction.

Because unlike poles attract, if you used the north pole of the magnet, the south pole of the nail will touch the magnet, and the other end of the nail will be the north pole. This means that, even if several nails are used, the free end of the last nail will have the same polarity as the pole that was used on the magnet.

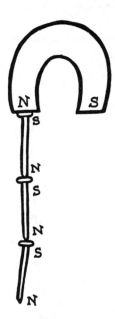

Fig. 22-1. *The permanent magnet induces a magnetic field in each of the nails.*

Experiment 23

Floating Needle

Materials

- ☐ needle with about a foot of thread
- ☐ horseshoe magnet

Magnetize the needle over one of the poles of the magnet. Then carefully lift the needle by the thread from this pole. The needle will keep pointing at that pole (Fig. 23-1). Now, still holding the end of the thread, try to lay the needle across the other pole of the magnet. If you move slowly, you will be able to position the needle so that it floats in the air above the other pole as shown in Fig. 23-2. The needle is suspended in the balance between the attraction of one pole and the repulsion of the other.

Fig. 23-1. *Suspend the magnetized needle over one of the poles of the magnet.*

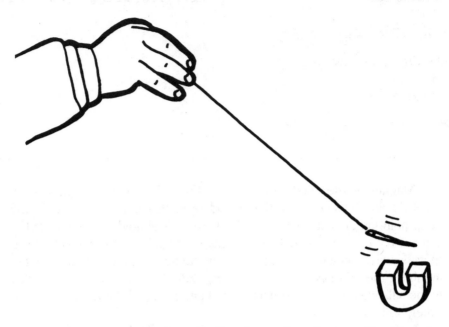

Fig. 23-2. *Careful positioning will allow the needle to float over the other pole.*

Experiment 24

Materials

- [ ] magnetized hacksaw blade
- [ ] hammer
- [ ] hot stove
- [ ] tongs or pliers

How to Destroy a Magnet

Strike the magnet with the hammer several times (Fig. 24-1). This will cause it to lose it's magnetism. Heating will also cause a magnet to lose it's power. The atoms in a magnet are aligned in the same direction. Hitting or heating will jumble the atoms, and they lose their alignment and the magnetic field disappears (Fig. 24-2). Try this experiment over a heated stove top with a magnetized blade (Fig. 24-3). Have an adult help, and use tongs or pliers so you can't burn your fingers.

Fig. 24-1. *A magnet can be destroyed by striking it with a hammer.*

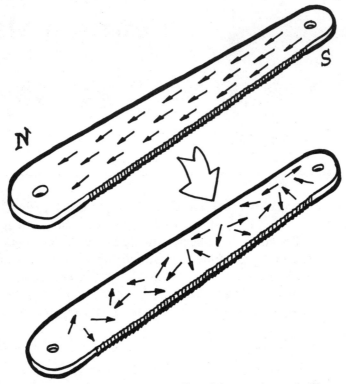

Fig. 24-2. *The atoms in a magnet are aligned from end to end. The steel has no magnetic field if the atoms are in a jumble.*

Fig. 24-3. *A magnet can be destroyed by heat.*

Experiment 25

Identifying the Poles of a Magnet

Materials

- ☐ magnet
- ☐ compass or suspended magnetized needle

Bring one of the poles near one end of the suspended needle. If a horseshoe magnet is used, a nail will have to be extended from the pole of the magnet (Fig. 25-1). This is because the two poles are too close together to get accurate results. The end of the needle that points north is really the south pole of the needle. It points north because it is the north-seeking end of the needle. Using the law that like poles repel and unlike poles attract, if the pole of the magnet is attracted to the end of the needle pointing north (south pole of needle), it is a north pole.

Fig. 25-1. *The magnetized south pole of the compass needle is the end that points north.*

Experiment 26

Dividing a Magnet

Materials

- ☐ magnetized hacksaw blade
- ☐ compass or suspended magnetized needle
- ☐ piece of heavy cloth

Test each end of the magnet to determine what the poles are. Mark the poles with a piece of chalk or a pencil (Fig. 26-1). Wrap the heavy cloth around the hacksaw blade and break it in half (Fig. 26-2). Check each half with the compass to see what happened to the poles. You will see you now have two complete magnets (Fig. 26-3). No matter how many times you divide the magnet, each half becomes a magnet with a north and south pole.

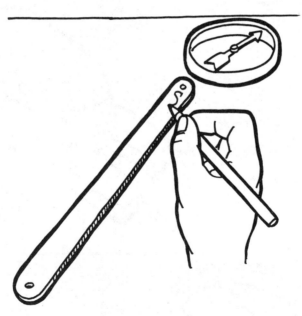

Fig. 26-1. *Mark the poles on a magnetized hacksaw blade.*

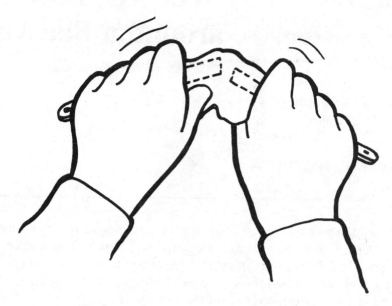

Fig. 26-2. *Carefully break the blade in half.*

Fig. 26-3. *Each piece of the blade has a north and south pole.*

Experiment 27

The Magnetic Field around a Bar Magnet

Materials

- ☐ bar magnet
- ☐ iron filings
- ☐ smooth, white cardboard or cardboard and white paper

Place the magnet on a table and lay the card over it. Gently sprinkle the iron filings over the card. You can make iron filings by filing a nail over the card (Fig. 27-1) or you can get them from a machine shop and use an old salt shaker to spread them. Filings from a machine shop should be washed in warm soapy water to remove the oil. Notice that some of the

Fig. 27-1. *Sprinkle iron filings on top of the card.*

filings grouped together and are standing on end, while others are scattered evenly about the card. Gently tap the card with your finger as shown in Fig. 27-2. Closer filings move into the group and leave an empty space, while the outer filings line up and form curved lines between the poles. There are the magnetic lines of force between the poles making up the magnetic field.

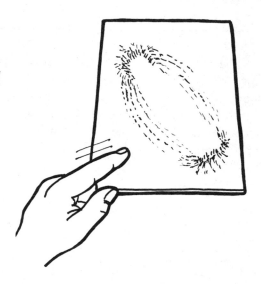

Fig. 27-2. *Tap the card and the filings will outline the magnetic field of a bar magnet.*

Experiment 28

The Magnetic Field around a Horseshoe Magnet

Materials

- ☐ horseshoe magnet
- ☐ iron filings
- ☐ smooth, white cardboard
  or cardboard and white
  paper

Place the horseshoe magnet flat on a table and lay the card on top (Fig. 28-1). Gently sprinkle the iron filings evenly over the card as shown in Fig. 28-2. Many of the filings will collect near each of the poles. Gently tap the card and some of the filings will form curved lines between the poles while the remaining ones will extend outward and form an outline of the lower part of the horseshoe (see Fig. 28-3).

Fig. 28-1. *Place a smooth white card over the horseshoe magnet.*

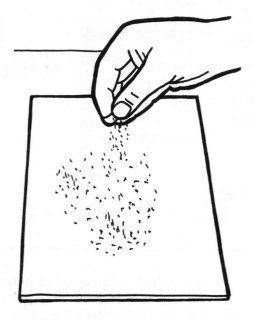

Fig. 28-2. *Sprinkle iron filings on top of the card.*

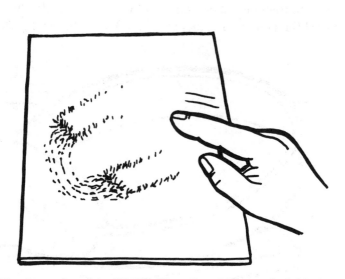

Fig. 28-3. *Tap the card and the filings will outline the magnetic field of a horseshoe magnet.*

Experiment 29

Tracing a Magnetic Field with a Floating Magnet

Materials

- [ ] small, magnetized needle
- [ ] cork disk (about 1/4 inch thick and 1 inch in diameter)
- [ ] large dish or aluminum pie pan
- [ ] water
- [ ] bar magnet

If the magnet is strong, place it under the dish. If you are using a piece of magnetized hacksaw blade place it in the dish. Fill the dish with about one inch of water (see Figs. 29-1 and 29-2). Push the magnetized needle through the center of the cork so that about a half inch of the needle sticks through (see Fig. 29-3). The needle should float in an upright position with the pointed end down. Lower this end into the water off to one side of the pole of the magnet (Fig. 29-4). If the end of the needle is

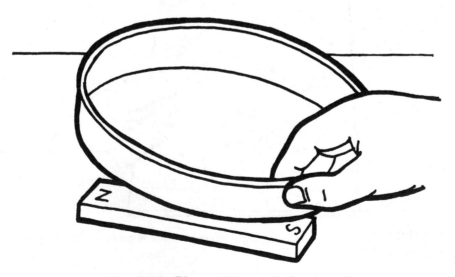

Fig. 29-1. *Place a dish over the bar magnet.*

Fig. 29-2. *Pour in a little water.*

Fig. 29-3. *Press the magnet-ized needle through the cork.*

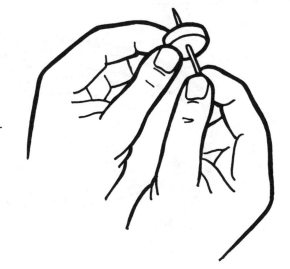

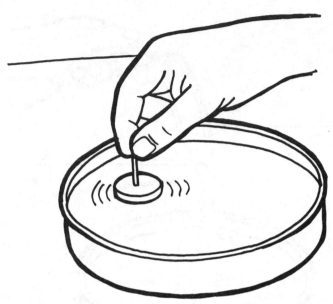

Fig. 29-4. *Float the needle near the end of one of the poles of the magnet.*

of the same polarity of the pole, the cork will float in an arc around to the other end of the magnet (Fig. 29-5). Try different starting positions and you will see the floating magnet trace out the curved lines of the magnetic field of the bar magnet.

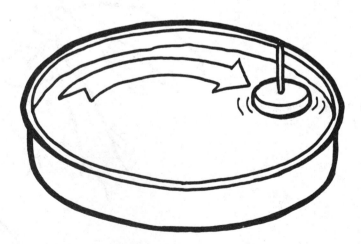

Fig. 29-5. *If the needle and the pole of the magnet has the same polarity, the needle will travel in an arc to the other pole of the magnet.*

Experiment 30

Tracing the Lines of Force with a Compass

Materials

☐ magnet
☐ compass

Bring the compass near the south pole of the magnet (Fig. 30-1). The needle will point away from the pole. Now slowly move the compass in the direction of the needle (Fig. 30-2). The compass will follow a curved path to the other pole of the magnet. This traces the lines of force of the magnetic field between the two poles.

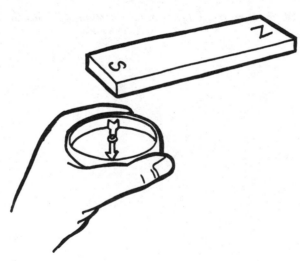

Fig. 30-1. *Place the compass near the south pole of the magnet.*

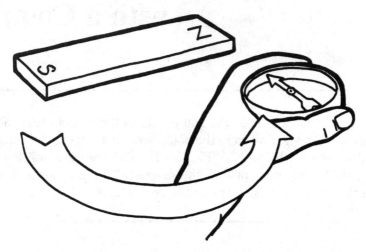

Fig. 30-2. *Move the compass in the direction of the needle.*

Experiment 31

How to Shield from a Magnetic Field

Materials

- ☐ two bar magnets (magnetized hacksaw blades)
- ☐ iron filings
- ☐ large, iron washer
- ☐ transparent tape
- ☐ glue
- ☐ smooth, white cardboard

Place the magnets about two or three inches apart in a line on the cardboard with the south pole of one magnet pointing toward the north pole of the other one (Fig. 31-1). Tape the magnets in place. Sprinkle iron filings in the space between the two poles as shown in Fig. 31-2.

Fig. 31-1. *Place the magnets on the card with the poles opposite each other.*

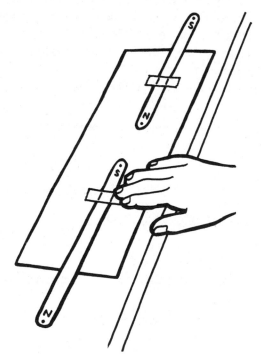

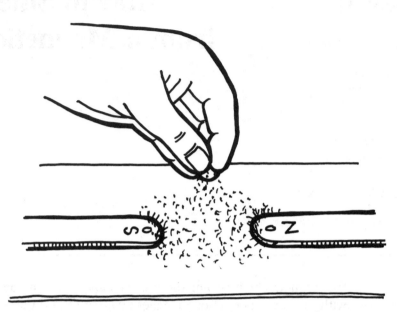

Fig. 31-2. *Sprinkle iron filings between the poles.*

Gently tap the cardboard. Notice the pattern of curved lines made by the filings (Fig. 31-3). Remove the iron filings and glue the washer in the center of the space (Fig. 31-4). Allow the glue to dry then sprinkle iron filings between the two magnets and tap the card (Fig. 31-5). Notice the pattern and that the filings inside the washer didn't line up. The iron washer shielded the filings inside against the magnetic field.

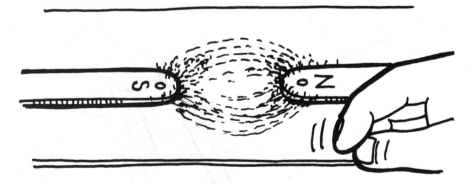

Fig. 31-3. *Tap the card to align the filings with the magnetic field.*

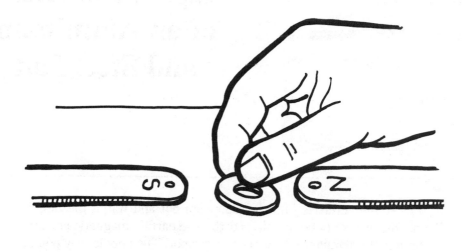

Fig. 31-4. *Remove the filings and glue the washer in place.*

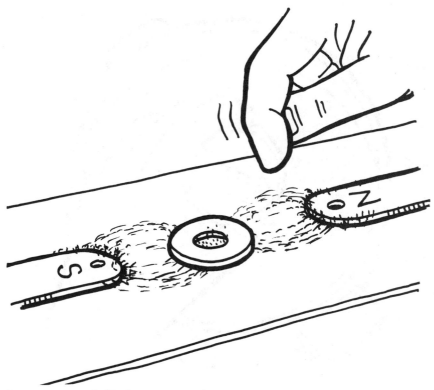

Fig. 31-5. *Sprinkle filings and notice the different pattern.*

Experiment 32

Magnetic Shielding of an Aluminum and Steel Pan

Materials

- ☐ compass (suspended magnetized needle)
- ☐ aluminum pot
- ☐ iron pot

Lower the compass into the aluminum pot and watch the needle. The needle will continue pointing north. The earth's magnetic lines travel through the aluminum. Now try the iron pot. The needle may point in any direction or could even swing back and forth (Fig. 32-1). The Earth's magnetic lines did not pass through the iron pot.

Fig. 32-1. *Place the compass inside the iron pot. The compass does not work.*

Experiment 33

Tracing the Earth's Magnetic Field

Materials

☐ paper
☐ pencil
☐ ruler
☐ compass (suspended
  magnetized needle)
☐ magnetized knitting needle

Draw a circle the diameter of the knitting needle to represent the earth (Fig. 33-1). Make a mark at the top and bottom to show the north and south poles (Fig. 33-2). Place the magnetized needle on these marks with the north end of the needle at the earth's North Pole. Place

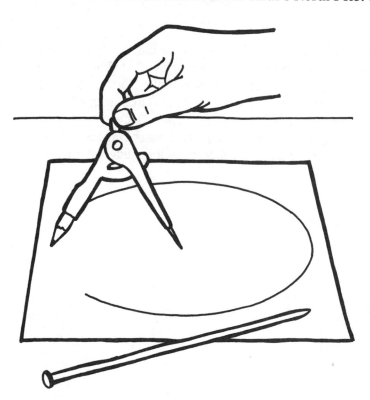

Fig. 33-1. *Draw a circle to represent the Earth.*

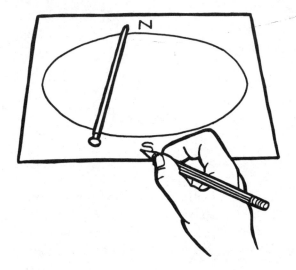

Fig. 33-2. *Mark the north and south poles.*

the compass near the earth's South Pole and slowly move it in the direction pointed by the needle as shown in Fig. 33-3. The compass will travel in a circular path from the South Pole to the North Pole. This is the pattern of the earth's magnetic field. The earth's magnetic axis is not the same as the true north-south axis. The magnetic pole is located at 76 degrees north latitude and 102 degrees west longitude. The true North Pole is 0 degrees latitude by 0 degrees longitude.

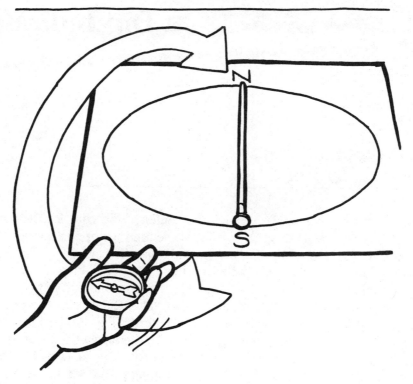

Fig. 33-3. *Place the magnetized needle on the poles and trace the magnetic field with the compass.*

Experiment 34

How to Make a Dip Indicator

Materials

- ☐ 2 needles (one longer than the other)
- ☐ drinking glass
- ☐ magnet
- ☐ cork

Push the long needle through the center of the cork for the east-west axis as shown in Fig. 34-1. Then shove the shorter one through the center of the cork for the north-south direction as shown in Fig. 34-2. They must balance with the short needle level when placed on the rim of the glass (see Fig. 34-3). Next, magnetize one end of the short needle with the north pole of the magnet. This should give the needle point a south pole that will make it point north (Fig. 34-4). Place the cork and needles on the rim of the glass with the magnetized end of the short needle pointing north. The needle should dip, showing that the earth's magnetic field has lines that pass through the earth to the North Pole (see Fig. 34-5). The angle of dip will become greater traveling northward. There will be no dip at the magnetic equator.

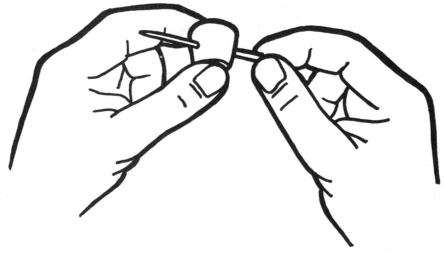

Fig. 34-1. *Push the longer needle through the cork.*

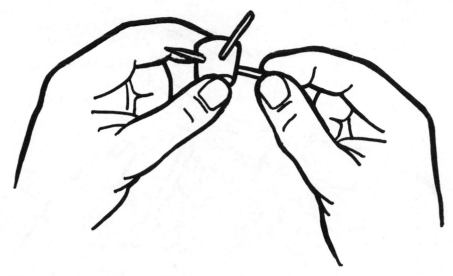

Fig. 34-2. *Force the second needle through the cork.*

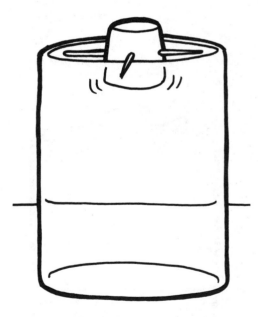

Fig. 34-3. *Balance the longer needle across the rim of the glass.*

Fig. 34-4. *Magnetize one end of the short needle with the north pole of the magnet.*

Fig. 34-5. *The needle will dip along the angle of the Earth's magnetic field.*

Experiment 35

Materials

- ☐ compass
- ☐ steel rod
- ☐ hammer
- ☐ patch of dirt outdoors

Magnetizing with the Earth's Magnetic Field

Using the compass, locate and mark a north-south line in the dirt (Fig. 35-1). Hold the rod in one hand over the line with the north end angled down about 60 degrees and against the ground. With a sharp rap, hit the south end of the rod with the hammer as shown in Fig. 35-2. If you were successful, the rod will be magnetized. The sharp rap aligned the molecules in the rod with the earth's magnetic field.

Fig. 35-1. *Mark a north-south line in the dirt.*

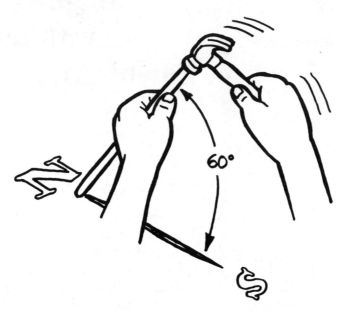

Fig. 35-2. *Place the steel rod against the dirt at an angle and strike it with a hammer.*

Experiment 36

How to Magnetize a Screwdriver

Leave a length of wire for a lead, then wrap the wire around the shank of the screwdriver in even coils (see Fig. 36-1). Use all of the wire except for another short length for a lead. Remove the insulation from the ends of the leads (see Fig. 36-2). Briefly touch the ends to the terminals of the battery (see Fig. 36-3). This should magnetize the screwdriver. The magnetic field of the coil aligns the molecules of the screwdriver into a magnet.

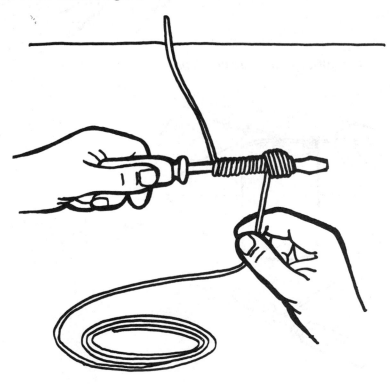

Fig. 36-1. *Wrap the wire around the screwdriver.*

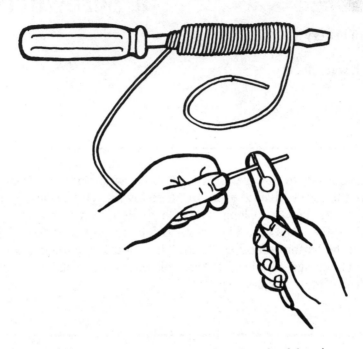

Fig. 36-2. *Strip the insulation from both ends of the wire.*

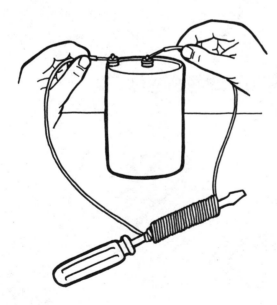

Fig. 36-3. *Briefly touch the wires to the battery.*

Experiment 37

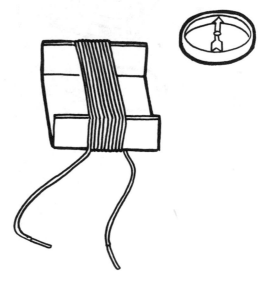

How to Make a Galvanometer

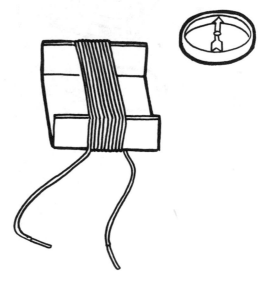

Materials

- ☐ compass
- ☐ flashlight battery
- ☐ 3 × 4 inch piece of cardboard
- ☐ insulated wire (bell wire)

Fold two ends of the cardboard up to form supports for the wire, then wrap the wire around the cardboard about 30 times (Fig. 37-1). Leave about a foot of surplus wire for connections. Scrape about a half inch of the insulation from each end. Place the compass on the cardboard and beneath the wire as shown in Fig. 37-2. Turn the cardboard so that the wires run east and west then connect them to the battery (Fig. 37-3). When the ends of the wires are connected to the battery, the compass needle will be deflected nearly east and west, showing the current flow. The galvanometer is a meter that can detect very small amounts of current and voltage.

Fig. 37-1. *Wrap the wire around the cardboard and remove the insulation from the ends.*

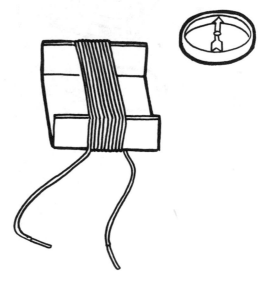

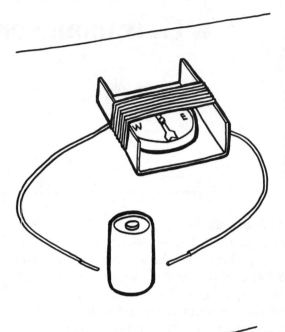

Fig. 37-2. *Place the compass inside the coil of wire. Align the wires east and west.*

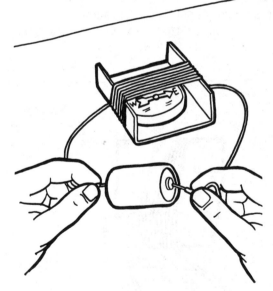

Fig. 37-3. *Touch the wires to the battery and watch the compass needle.*

Experiment 38

Induced Current from a Magnet

Materials

☐ bar magnet
☐ insulated wire (bell wire)
☐ galvanometer
  (see Experiment 37)

Wrap the wire around your fingers about 30 times to make a coil as shown in Fig. 38-1. It should be a little larger than the bar magnet. Leave a length free at each end to make connections. Remove about a half inch of the insulation on each end and connect them to the galvanometer (see Fig. 38-2). Move the bar magnet abruptly in and out of the center of the coil as shown in Fig. 38-3.

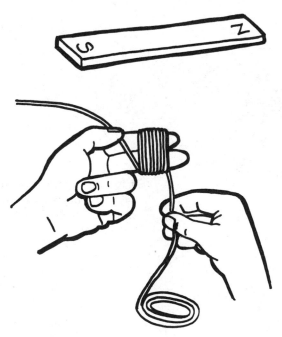

Fig. 38-1. *Make a coil of wire.*

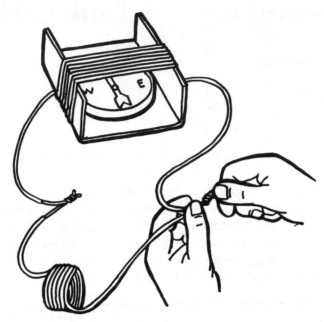

Fig. 38-2. *Connect the coil to the coil with the compass.*

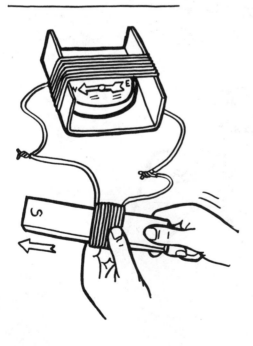

Fig. 38-3. *Quickly push the magnet into the coil and watch the compass needle.*

Notice the direction of the movement of the needle. When the magnet is first pushed into the coil, the needle is deflected in one direction and then in the other direciton when the magnet is removed. The current changed directions (Fig. 38-4). The current can be increased by using a stronger magnet, moving the magnet faster, or adding more loops in the coil.

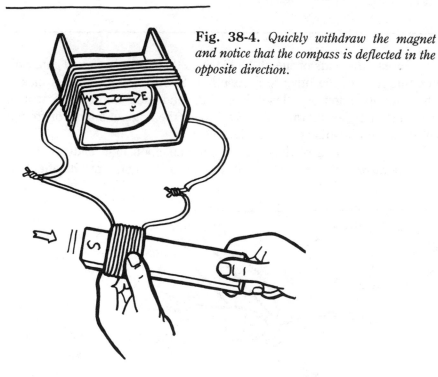

Fig. 38-4. *Quickly withdraw the magnet and notice that the compass is deflected in the opposite direction.*

Experiment 39

Induced Current in a Closed Loop

Spread the ends of one of the loops so that there is a small gap. Solder the ends of the other loop together. See Figure 39-1. This makes one open loop and one closed loop. Suspend each loop by two strings from a support as shown in Fig. 39-2 (over the edge of a table or from a ruler between two stacks of books, etc.).

Insert one end of the magnet into the open loop and watch the movement of the loop as shown in Fig. 39-3. It should not be affected.

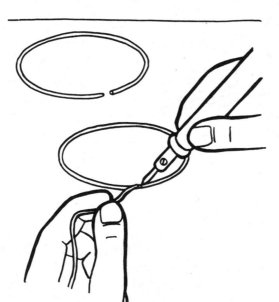

Fig. 39-1. *Solder the ends of one of the loops together.*

92

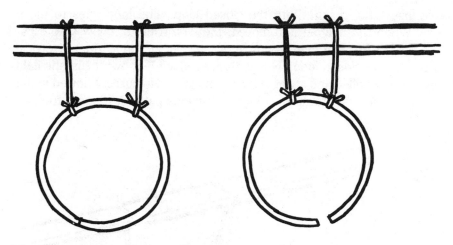

Fig. 39-2. *Suspend the loops from a support.*

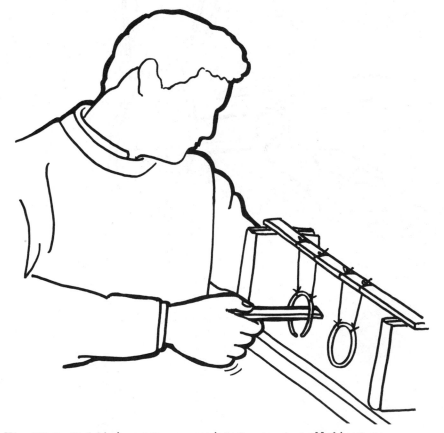

Fig. 39-3. *Quickly insert the magnet into the open loop. Nothing happens.*

Now insert the magnet into the closed loop. The loop tries to move away. When the magnet is removed, the loop tries to follow (see Figs. 39-4 and 39-5). The magnetic field of the magnet induced an electrical current in the closed loop. This current produced its own magnetic field which was repelled and attracted to the magnet. No current flowed in the open loop because there must be a continuous path for current to flow.

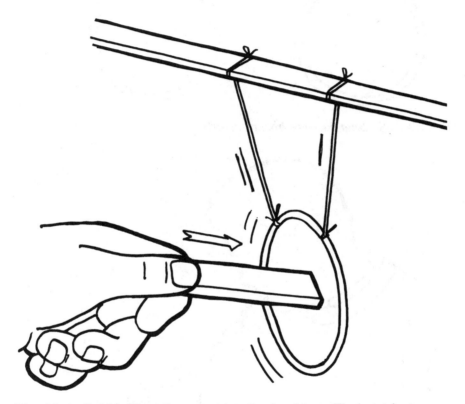

Fig. 39-4. *Quickly insert the magnet into the closed loop. The loop tries to move away.*

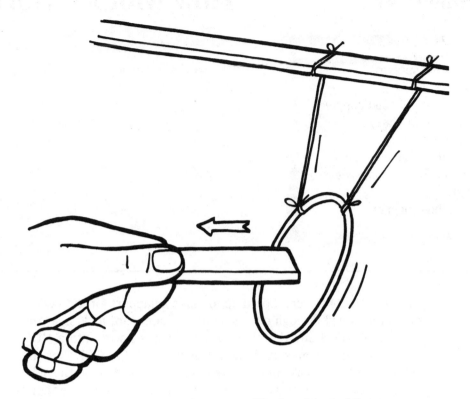

Fig. 39-5. *Quickly withdraw the magnet. The loop tries to follow.*

How Motors Work

Materials

- [ ] cardboard support
- [ ] pencil
- [ ] short piece of solid copper or aluminum wire
- [ ] flashlight battery
- [ ] 2 lengths of small copper wire (each about two feet long)
- [ ] horseshoe magnet

Fold the ends of the cardboard up to make a support for the pencil, then press the pencil through each side of the cardboard folds near the top (see Fig. 40-1). Bend the short piece of copper wire into a "U" shape, with the ends bent out about 1/4 inch (see Fig. 40-2). Now tie one end of one of the small copper wires tightly to the bend in the solid copper wire. Connect the end of the other copper wire to the other bend the same way (see Fig. 40-3). Loop the wires over the pencil a couple of

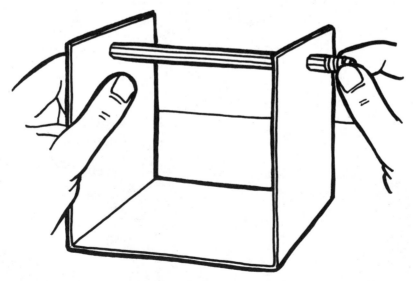

Fig. 40-1. *Force the pencil through the ends of the cardboard.*

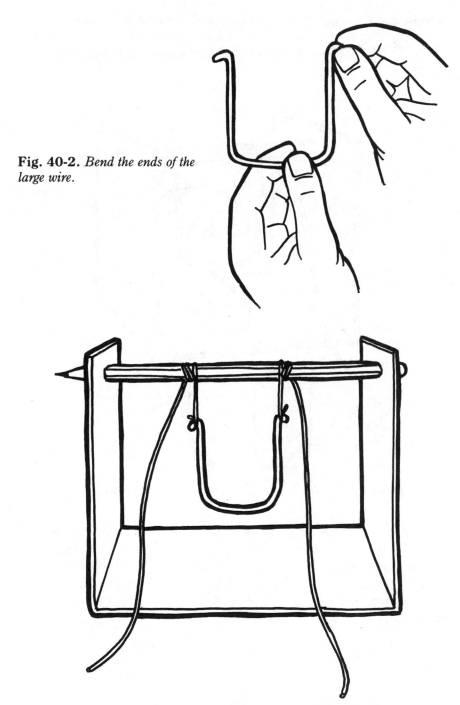

Fig. 40-2. *Bend the ends of the large wire.*

Fig. 40-3. *Suspend the large copper "U" by the fine copper wire.*

times so that the copper "U" is suspended from the pencil like a swing as shown in Fig. 40-4. Position the horseshoe magnet on it's side so that the copper "U" is free to swing between the poles of the magnet (see Fig. 40-5).

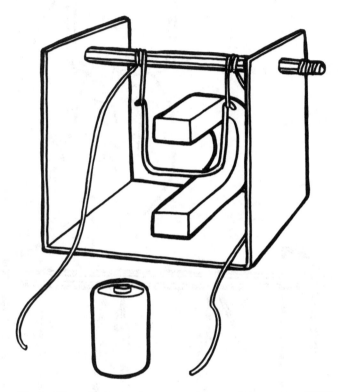

Fig. 40-4. *Place the horseshoe magnet around the copper "U".*

Connect the ends of the small copper wire to the battery. The copper "U" will swing out or in depending on which way the current flows. To change directions, swap ends of the battery. When the current flows through the copper "U," it becomes an electromagnet and it is attracted or repelled from the magnet. This is the principle that makes a motor operate.

Fig. 40-5. *Touch the ends of the wires to the battery.*

Experiment 41

The Pulling Wires

Materials

- ☐ 2 × 4 piece of lumber (about two feet long)
- ☐ small, copper wire (about 10 feet long)
- ☐ 2 combs (rubber or plastic)
- ☐ 2 small nails
- ☐ battery and two lead wires
- ☐ hand saw
- ☐ hammer

Have an adult help you cut out a notch across the wood near each end to hold the combs (see Fig. 41-1). Drive a nail part way into the wood at each end of the board to hold the wire. Place a comb in each slot

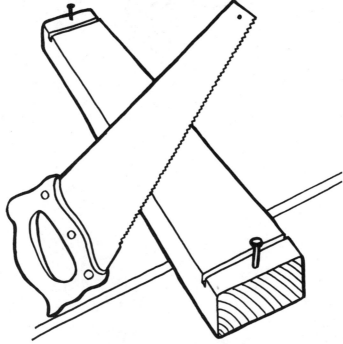

Fig. 41-1. *Cut the slots and drive two nails part-way into the board.*

with the teeth pointing up and string the wire between the two nails using the teeth in the combs to separate each strand (see Fig. 41-2). You should have about four strands.

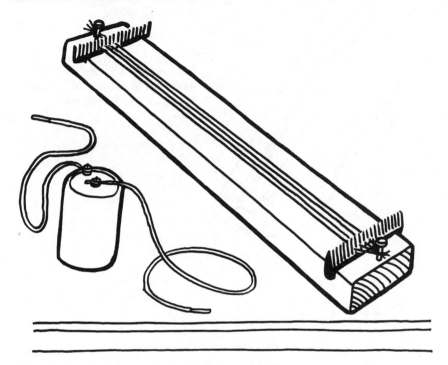

Fig. 41-2. *String the wire between the two nails.*

Connect the lead wires from the battery to each nail. The wires will pull toward each other (Fig. 41-3). When the current flows in the same direction through parallel wires, the magnetic fields they develop are attracted to each other.

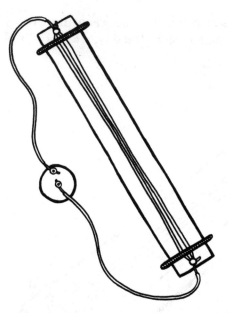

Fig. 41-3. *Connect the lead wires to the battery and notice how the wires pull together.*

Experiment 42

Materials

- ☐ 1/4 inch iron bolt (about three inches long)
- ☐ 1/4 inch nut and 2 washers
- ☐ battery
- ☐ small, insulated copper wire (about three feet long)

How to Make an Electromagnet

Place one of the washers on the bolt and, leaving a few inches of wire for a lead, wrap about 50 turns around the bolt as shown in Figs. 42-1 and 42-2. Leave a little wire at the end for another lead and slide the other washer over the bolt. Screw the nut in place (Fig. 42-3). This is an electromagnet. When the ends of the coil are connected to a battery, the electromagnet can pick up small nails and paper clips as shown in Fig. 42-4.

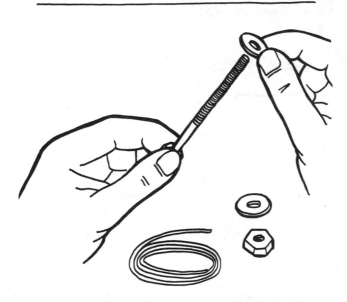

Fig. 42-1. *Place the washer onto the bolt.*

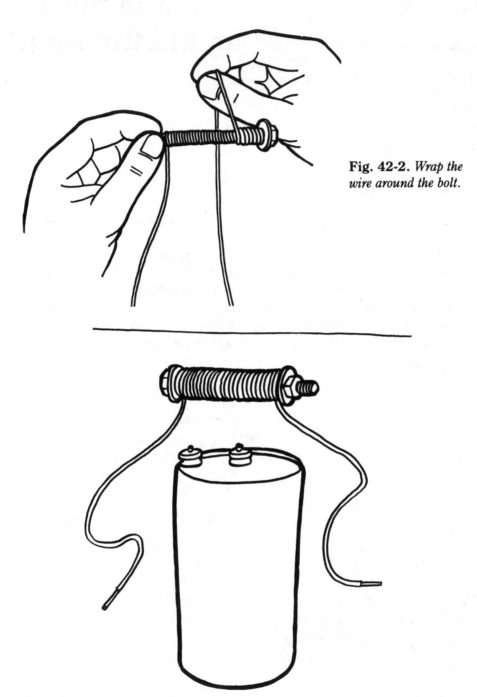

Fig. 42-2. *Wrap the wire around the bolt.*

Fig. 42-3. *Connect the wires to the battery and the electromagnet will pick up small nails.*

Fig. 42-4. *Connect the wires to the battery and the electromagnet will pick up small nails.*

Experiment 43

The Dancing Figure

Cut out the head and body from the thin cardboard and make the arms and legs by stringing paper clips to the body (see Fig. 43-1). Cut a large square opening in the side of the box near the bottom for the stage opening as shown in Fig. 43-2. Suspend the figure from the top of the box by the thread, making sure the figure is centered in the stage opening. Tape the electromagnet to the top of the box and run the leads out the side (see Fig. 43-3). Connect and disconnect the leads to the battery and the figure appears to dance (Fig. 43-4).

The electromagnet attracts the paper clips when the current is on and they fall back in place when the current is off.

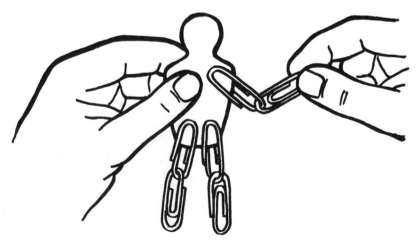

Fig. 43-1. *Use paper clips for the arms and legs.*

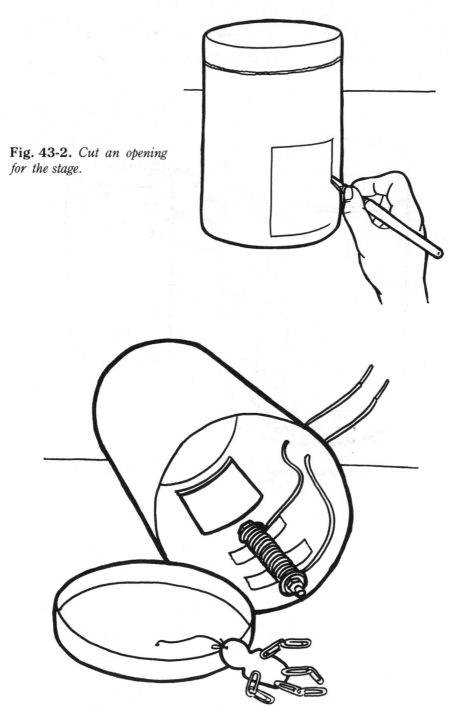

Fig. 43-2. *Cut an opening for the stage.*

Fig. 43-3. *Tape the electromagnet in place and suspend the figure from the lid.*

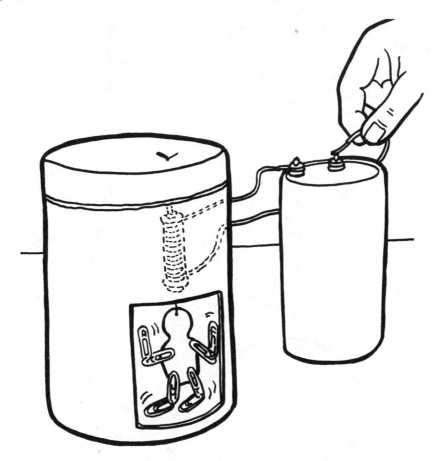

Fig. 43-4. *Briefly touch the wires to the battery to make the figure dance.*

Experiment 44

Materials

- ☐ battery
- ☐ electromagnet
  (see Experiment 42)
- ☐ two pieces of small,
  insulated copper wire
  (about three feet long)
- ☐ wooden dowel or yardstick
- ☐ transparent tape
- ☐ string
- ☐ few paper clips or small
  nails

Using the string, attach the electromagnet to the end of the yardstick with one end of the magnet pointing down (Fig. 44-1). Strip about a half inch of insulation from the ends of the copper wire. Twist one of the

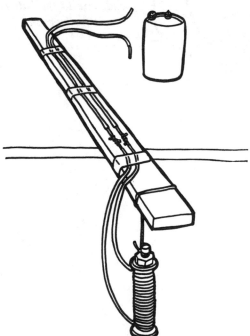

Fig. 44-1. *Suspend the elecromagnet from the yardstick.*

leads of the electromagnet to one end of the copper wire. Connect the other lead the same way. Run the wires down the yardstick and tape them in a couple of places to keep them in place as shown in Fig. 44-1. Connect one of the wires to one of the terminals of the battery. Hold the yardstick and lower the magnet near one of the paper clips or nails. Touch the other wire to the other terminal of the battery and the magnet will pick up the paper clips or nails as shown in Fig. 44-2. Remove the wire from the battery, and the items will fall.

The iron bolt becomes magnetized when an electrical current is flowing, but when the current stops, it loses it's magnetism.

Fig. 44-2. *Touch the lead wire to the battery to operate the crane.*

Experiment 45

How to Make an Electromagnetic Relay

Materials

- ☐ 2, 1-1/2 volt batteries
- ☐ 1, 1-1/2 volt bulb
- ☐ electromagnet (see Experiment 42)
- ☐ insulated copper wire
- ☐ mounting board (about 12 inches square)
- ☐ 2 metal contact strips (copper or aluminum)
- ☐ 2 thumbtacks
- ☐ small nail
- ☐ popsicle stick
- ☐ transparent tape

Mount the electromagnet on its side to the mounting board with tape. Refer to the electromagnetic relay in Fig. 45-1 to help you visualize the set-up instructions. Use tape to connect one of the lead wires to one of the batteries. Push a thumb tack in each end of the popsicle stick, but on opposite sides. Drive the nail into the mounting board, and tape the center of the stick to the nail. This will be a pivot point. It should be mounted so that one end is against the end of the electromagnet and the other end presses the contacts together.

Bend one end of the contact strips up and mount it on the board using screws. Bend the other contact strip to make a square loop over the first strip. Mount it on the board. Connect a wire from one of the contacts to one end of the other battery. Connect a wire from the other end of the battery to the bottom contact on the bulb. Run a wire from the metal side of the bulb back to the other contact strip. You can twist the wire around the side of the bulb and use tape to hold the wire to the bottom. If a soldering iron is available, use solder to make the connections.

When the lead from the electromagnet is touched to its battery, the stick pivots and closes the contacts, and the bulb lights. Relays are used when a small voltage is used to control a larger voltage in a second separate circuit.

111

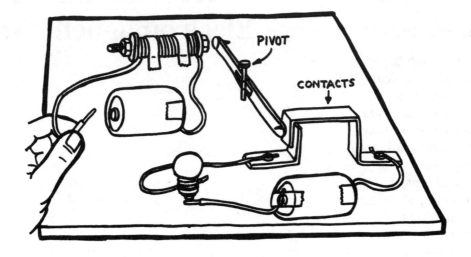

Fig. 45-1. *The electromagnet can be used as a relay to operate another circuit.*

Experiment 46

How to Make a Simple Telegraph

Materials

- ☐ battery
- ☐ 20 feet of insulated copper wire (bell wire)
- ☐ 2 nails with large heads
- ☐ 3 or 4 small nails
- ☐ 3 pieces of one inch thick wood (4 × 8, 4 × 4, and 2 × 4 inch)
- ☐ thin sheet of tin such as the bottom of a coffee can (not aluminum)
- ☐ tin snips
- ☐ transparent tape
- ☐ 3 small screws

To make a switch, cut a strip of tin about 1 × 3 inches. Use one of the screws to mount one end of the strip to the 2 × 4 inch board, but don't tighten it. The strip should run lengthwise down the top of the board (Fig. 46-1). Near the other end of the board, drive another screw part way in. The free end of the tin strip should lap over this screw. Set

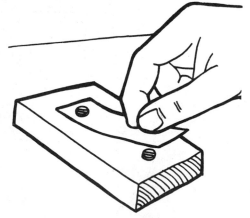

Fig. 46-1. *The switch is simply two contacts.*

the switch aside until later. Next, using small nails, attach the 4 × 4 inch board on top of, and flush with, one end of the 4 × 8 inch board (Fig. 46-2). Drive the two large nails in about two inches apart near the end of the bottom board.

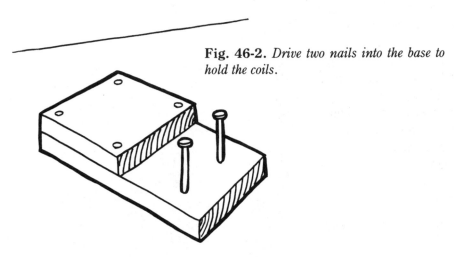

Fig. 46-2. *Drive two nails into the base to hold the coils.*

Before you begin to wire the telegraph, leave about 18 inches of wire free for a lead. Facing the end with the two nails, begin winding at the bottom of the right nail (Fig. 46-3). Make about 20 turns. Try to wind the wire as tightly as possible. When you reach the top, keep the wire tight and start winding at the bottom of the nail on the left. Once

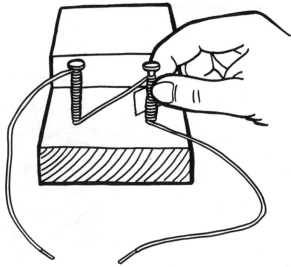

Fig. 46-3. *Wrap the wire around the nails and hold in place with tape.*

you're done winding the wires, hold them in place with transparent tape. This is an electromagnet.

Connect the wire to one of the screws of the switch and tighten the screw. Connect another wire from the other screw to one of the battery terminals. Connect the other wire from the electromagnet to the other battery terminal. Cut a "T" shaped piece from the tin. The top of the "T" must fit over the top of the two nails (Fig 46-5). Use a screw to attach the bottom end of the "T" to the top board as shown in Fig. 46-4. Bend a curve in the "T" so that the top is level across, and just above the two nails. The telegraph is complete.

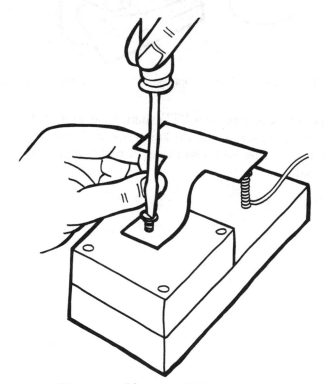

Fig. 46-4. *Mount the "T" to the base.*

Press down on the switch and the "T" on the other board will make a click. When the switch is released the "T" snaps back.

The switch is the telegraph key. This opens and closes the circuit. The large board with the metal "T" is the receiver. When the key is pressed, the current flows through the electromagnet. This creates a

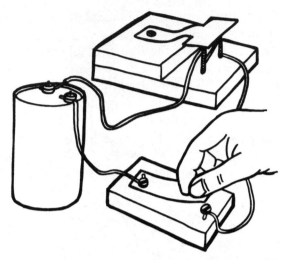

Fig. 46-5. *Connect the battery and operate the telegraph with the switch.*

magnetic field that attracts the "T" shaped piece of metal to the nail heads and causes a click. When the key is released, the circuit is broken and the metal T snaps back into place. A real telegraph works on the same principle.

Experiment 47

How to Make an Electric Lock

Materials

☐ large nail with the head
  cut off
☐ battery
☐ plastic straw
☐ small, u-shaped metal strap
  and two screws
☐ insulated copper wire (bell
  wire)
☐ small spring
☐ transparent tape

Wind the bell wire around the straw about 50 times. Leave a few inches sticking out at each end for leads. Cut of any excess straw and hold the coil in place with tape. The nail should slide freely inside the straw. This will be the solenoid. Mount this on the fixed part of the door or opening and securely fasten it in place so that the spring will only be strong enough to keep the nail extended when no power is applied. Mount the u-shaped strap to the moving part of the opening, the lid, or the door. Connect the leads from the coil to a battery and the lock will open (see Fig. 47-1). A hidden remote pushbutton switch is used on locks like this in high security areas such as banks and government agencies.

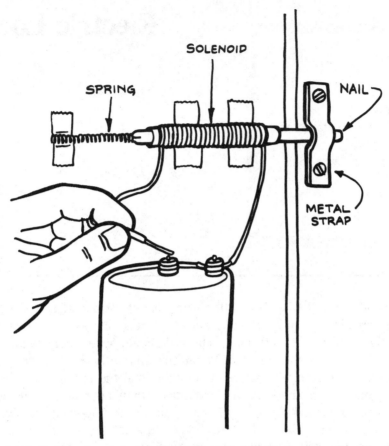

Fig. 47-1. *The electric lock is usually installed inside the door. The illustration shows how the lock works.*

Experiment 48

How to Make a Model Railroad Signal

Materials

- ☐ battery
- ☐ small copper wire (about 4 feet of bell wire)
- ☐ One-inch piece of wood (about eight inches long)
- ☐ string (about six inches long)
- ☐ wood base (three inches square)
- ☐ cardboard signal flag (about 2 × 1/4 inches)
- ☐ 3 one-inch nails
- ☐ 1, 1 1/2 inch nail
- ☐ metal strip (4 × 1/4 inches)

Drive the larger nail part way into the top of the wooden base. This will be the core of the electromagnet. Leave a length of wire for a lead and neatly wrap about 30 turns of wire around the nail. Leave a length of the wire at the other end for the second lead. Nail one end of the metal strip to the side of the base and bend it in a curve, so that the other end is a little above and slightly past the head of the nail (Fig. 48-1). Push a nail through the signal flag about a half inch from the end and attach it near one end of the eight-inch piece of wood (Fig. 48-2). Nail the other end of the wood to the side of the base opposite the metal strip. Tie one end of the string to the short end of the signal flag and the other end to the metal strip (Fig. 48-3). Adjust the length of the string so that the flag will stick straight out when the metal strip is pressed to the head of the nail (Fig. 48-4). The flag should hang down when the strip is released.

When the leads are connected to the battery, the electromagnet pulls down the metal strip. The attached string pulls down the short end of the flag which makes the longer end pivot straight out. When one of the leads is disconnected, the electromagnet loses it's magnetism and the flag drops.

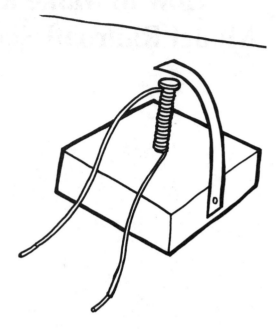

Fig. 48-1. *Mount the electro-magnet and contact on the base.*

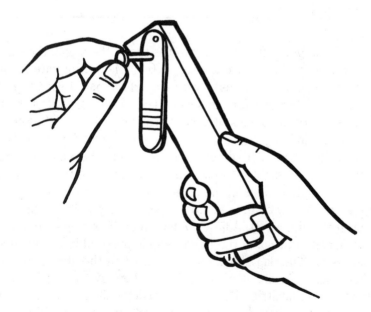

Fig. 48-2. *Attach the signal flag to it's support.*

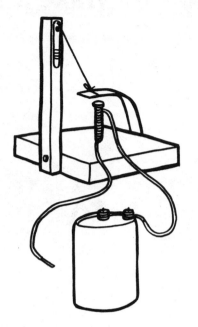

Fig. 48-3. *Mount the support to the base and connect the string between the flag and the contact.*

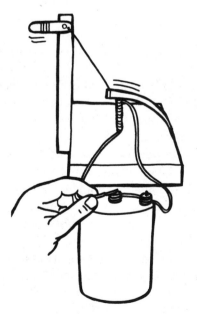

Fig. 48-4. *Touch the lead wire to the battery to operate the signal flag.*

Experiment 49

How to Make a Motor

With the hammer and nail, punch a hole a half inch from each end of the two metal strips. Bend one end of each strip about once inch from the end as shown in Fig. 49-1. This will be a foot for each support as shown in Fig. 49-1. Use the two screws and mount the strips on the wood base. The metal strips should be positioned so that the plastic knitting needle will fit through the two holes at the top of the strips as shown in Fig. 49-2. About one inch of the needle should stick past each support. The needle must be able to turn freely in it's support and the cork must be able to fit easily between the poles of the horseshoe magnet.

Insert the needle through one of the holes in the support and push it through the center of the cork from end to end. Wrap wire around the cork about 50 turns to form a coil as shown in Fig. 49-3. Leave about three inches for leads on each end. Remove about a half inch of insulation from the end of each lead and tape them to opposite sides of the needle. Do not let the bare wires touch each other and don't cover them with tape. The bare ends will be electrical contacts for the two wires from the battery. Push the two tacks part way into the wood base below

122

Fig. 49-1. *Bend the metal strips to form a support.*

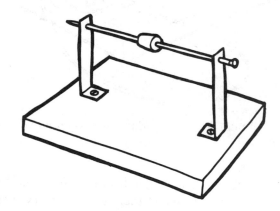

Fig. 49-2. *Install the plastic needle and cork on the supports.*

the contacts (bare ends of wire) as shown in Fig. 49-4. Remove about a half inch of insulation from another wire and bend it up from one of the tacks so that the bare end lays across the bare wire from the coil. Hold it in place with the tack. Remove about a half inch of insulation from another wire and mount it the same way except the end should lay across the other bare wire from the coil. Next, mount the magnet on the base so that the two ends of the magnet stick up on each side of the coil

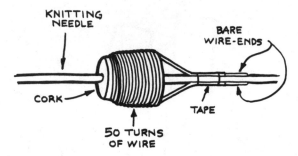

Fig. 49-3. *Wrap the wire around the cork.*

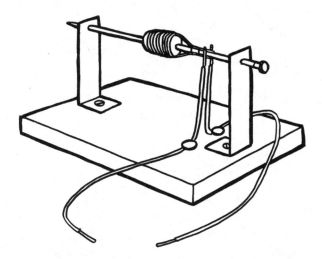

Fig. 49-4. *Mount the two lead wires. Make sure they can make contact with the bare ends of the coil.*

(Fig. 49-5). Remove about a half inch of insulation from the free ends of the wires held by the tacks. Connect them to the battery terminals and give the cork a spin with your hand. The motor should now spin by itself. Don't be discouraged if it doesn't work the first time. This is a difficult experiment and you might have to make adjustments to your motor.

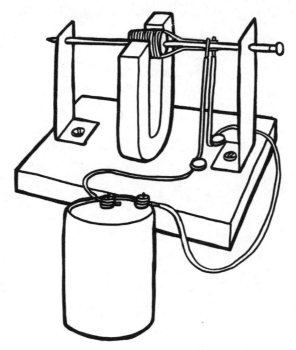

Fig. 49-5. *Attach the horseshoe magnet to the base and connect the lead wires to the battery.*

SCIENCE FAIR
PROJECTS

Science fairs are like parades. They can be fun and exciting, but they require careful planning. The most important part of entering a science fair is choosing a project. It should be something that you are really interested in. You will also want to keep the project within your abilities. Projects that are too complicated have a way of not getting completed. You will soon lose interest if the project becomes too difficult. Also, when you choose a project, be sure all of the materials you'll need are available. So take plenty of time to select a subject. Your project should be about a specific problem or question. For example, if the subject was magnets, you could try to answer what happens to the poles if the magnet is divided in half. No matter how many times a magnet is cut in half, scientist have been unable to separate one pole from the other.

Once you have selected a project, break it down into about three steps. For example, your project should: (1) Answer a question or have a hypothesis (a guess of what the results of an experiment will be); (2)

Fig. 1. *A panel can be used to explain your project.*

Completing the experiment; and (3) The results or conclusions of the experiment.

Most science fair projects include a report. This should explain why the experiment was done, the results of the experiment, and the conclusions. Graphs and charts can be helpful in presenting information. You might want to make a model of your project. In most cases, you can use wood or cardboard. Often, normal household throw-aways like wooden spools from thread, cardboard tubes from paper towels, coffee cans, and different shaped plastic and glass bottles can be used.

A project can be displayed on a table with a self-supporting panel for a background. Panels can be made of wood or stiff cardboard, divided into three sections with the ends folded forward at a slight angle. This enables the panel to stand by itself. The section on the left can display drawings with text explaining why the experiment was selected. The middle part can display the experiment and explain the steps you took, and the section on the right can show the results and conclusions of the experiment (see Fig. 1).

Try to make your project interesting. If you wanted to show how an electric crane works, you could build an electromagnet that is suspended by a pulley attached to a boom. The boom could be mounted on a platform that swiveled and traveled a short distance. This can be set in a model railroad or harbor to load and unload steel from trains and ships (see Fig. 2).

The experiment on how to make a circuit could be set up with a battery, switch, and a light to show that, for an electrical current to flow, it must travel in a closed loop. This begins at the battery, goes out through the load, and returns to the battery. The switch simply interrupts the flow. The display could show cartoon characters of electrons running from the negative terminal of the battery, through the switch, then the light and back to the positive terminal of the battery.

Be creative with your project and use your imagination. Most experiments have been done before, so it's not important to be first. You can use a different approach or have a different point of view. Use you own personal touch rather than following directions right out of a book. Electricity and magnetism have been around since the beginning of time. We still don't fully understand it, but by using a different approach to a basic problem, experimenters have made giant steps in the advancement of this exciting field.

Fig. 2. *Imagination is important when building your project.*

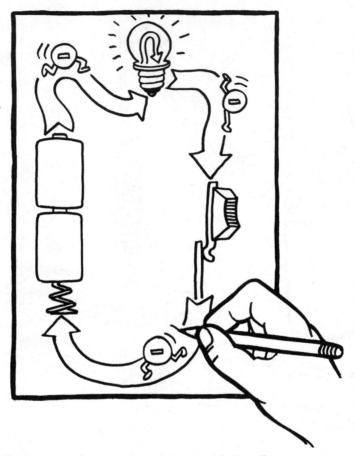

Fig. 3. *Try to be creative when you make your display. Electrons move, so it's important to show action.*

Index